MARVEL LEGACY

MARVEL LEGACY

MARVEL LEGACY #1

JASON AARON
WRITER

ESAD RIBIĆ WITH STEVE McNIVEN
ARTIST

MATTHEW WILSON
COLOR ARTIST

CHRIS SAMNEE; RUSSELL DAUTERMAN; ALEX MALEEV;
ED McGUINNESS; STUART IMMONEN & WADE VON GRAWBADGER;
PEPE LARRAZ; JIM CHEUNG; DANIEL ACUÑA; GREG LAND
& JAY LEISTEN; MIKE DEODATO JR. AND DAVID MARQUEZ
ADDITIONAL ARTISTS

VC's CORY PETIT
LETTERER

JOE QUESADA, KEVIN NOWLAN & RICHARD ISANOVE
COVER ART

ALANNA SMITH
ASSISTANT EDITOR

TOM BREVOORT
EDITOR

MARVEL PRIMERS

ROBBIE THOMPSON
WRITER

MARK BAGLEY, JOHN DELL, ANDREW HENNESSY, KEVIN LIBRANDA, DANIEL ACUÑA, EDGAR SALAZAR, ANTHONY PIPER, PERE PÉREZ, ALBERTO ALBURQUERQUE, JOE BENNETT, BELARDINO BRABO, VALERIO SCHITI, DAVID BALDEÓN, BRENT SCHOONOVER, WILFREDO TORRES, DAVID LOPEZ, MARCUS TO, TODD NAUCK, GERMÁN PERALTA, ROD REIS, DALIBOR TALAJIĆ, NIKO HENRICHON, MATT HORAK, MARCO FAILLA, NATHAN STOCKMAN, RON LIM, MARC DEERING, JORGE COELHO, ANDREA SORRENTINO, GREG LAND, JAY LEISTEN, VERONICA FISH, IBRAIM ROBERSON, DIEGO OLORTEGUI, CARLOS PACHECO & RAFAEL FONTERIZ
ARTISTS

RACHELLE ROSENBERG, CHRIS SOTOMAYOR, DONO SÁNCHEZ-ALMARA, DANIEL ACUÑA, ANTHONY PIPER, DAN BROWN, ISRAEL SILVA, ANDY TROY, JOSÉ VILLARRUBIA, RUTH REDMOND, EMILIO LOPEZ, FRANK D'ARMATA, RAIN BEREDO, JORDAN BOYD, IAN HERRING, JESUS ABURTOV, JIM CAMPBELL, MIROSLAV MRVA, NIKO HENRICHON, CHRIS O'HALLORAN, MIKE SPICER, ANTONIO FABELA, MARCIO MENYZ, LEE LOUGHRIDGE, ANDREA SORRENTINO, VERONICA FISH & EDGAR DELGADO
COLOR ARTISTS

VC's CLAYTON COWLES, CORY PETIT, TRAVIS LANHAM, JOE SABINO & JOE CARAMAGNA
LETTERERS

KATHLEEN WISNESKI
ASSISTANT EDITOR

DARREN SHAN
EDITOR

COLLECTION EDITOR JENNIFER GRÜNWALD ▪ ASSISTANT EDITOR CAITLIN O'CONNELL
ASSOCIATE MANAGING EDITOR KATERI WOODY ▪ EDITOR, SPECIAL PROJECTS MARK D. BEAZLEY
VP PRODUCTION & SPECIAL PROJECTS JEFF YOUNGQUIST ▪ SVP PRINT, SALES & MARKETING DAVID GABRIEL
BOOK DESIGNER JAY BOWEN

EDITOR IN CHIEF C.B. CEBULSKI ▪ CHIEF CREATIVE OFFICER JOE QUESADA
PRESIDENT DAN BUCKLEY ▪ EXECUTIVE PRODUCER ALAN FINE

MARVEL LEGACY. Contains material originally published in magazine form as MARVEL LEGACY #1 and FOOM MAGAZINE. First printing 2018. ISBN 978-1-302-91102-7. Published by MARVEL WORLDWIDE, INC., a subsidiary of MARVEL ENTERTAINMENT, LLC. OFFICE OF PUBLICATION: 135 West 50th Street, New York, NY 10020. Copyright © 2018 MARVEL No similarity between any of the names, characters, persons, and/or institutions in this magazine with those of any living or dead person or institution is intended, and any such similarity which may exist is purely coincidental. **Printed in the U.S.A.** DAN BUCKLEY, President, Marvel Entertainment; JOHN NEE, Publisher; JOE QUESADA, Chief Creative Officer; TOM BREVOORT, SVP of Publishing; DAVID BOGART, SVP of Business Affairs & Operations, Publishing & Partnership; DAVID GABRIEL, SVP of Sales & Marketing, Publishing; JEFF YOUNGQUIST, VP of Production & Special Projects; DAN CARR, Executive Director of Publishing Technology; ALEX MORALES, Director of Publishing Operations; DAN EDINGTON, Managing Editor; SUSAN CRESPI, Production Manager; STAN LEE, Chairman Emeritus. For information regarding advertising in Marvel Comics or on Marvel.com, please contact Vit DeBellis, Custom Solutions & Integrated Advertising Manager, at vdebellis@marvel.com. For Marvel subscription inquiries, please call 888-511-5480. **Manufactured between 6/8/2018 and 7/10/2018 by LSC COMMUNICATIONS INC., KENDALLVILLE, IN, USA.**

10 9 8 7 6 5 4 3 2 1

MARVEL LEGACY #1 VARIANT BY **ALEX ROSS**

OR WHOSE I SHOULD BE RUNNING FAR AWAY FROM.

GET THE HEL AWAY FROM MY *HAMMER!*

AAAK!

SORRY SON OF A DISEASED TROLL THAT IT IS.

MJOLNIR! YOU WERE SUPPOSED TO RETURN TO MY *BLASTED* HAND!

I WILL *BREAK* YOU, YOU STUBBORN HUNK OF URU.

I WILL BEND YOU TO MY WILL EVEN IF IT TAKES A MILLION--

YOU *LOST* IT AGAIN.

IT *SLIPPED* WAS ALL.

FOR AN *ALL-FATHER,* YOU ARE A TERRIBLE LIAR, *LORD ODIN.*

I THINK WHENEVER YOU THROW IT, THE HAMMER SEES IT AS AN OPPORTUNITY TO *ESCAPE.*

AND I THINK YOU SHOULD MIND YOUR OWN BOR-DAMNED BUSINESS.

YOUR PROFICIENCY IN BATTLE HAS BECOME MY BUSINESS, ASGARDIAN, WHETHER I LIKE IT OR NOT.

FOR THE *PHOENIX* DOES NOT PLAN ON DYING HERE TODAY.

DID YOU SEE THE MONSTER *FALL?*

DYING? DOES THIS LOOK LIKE VALHALLA? NAY, 'TIS STILL JUST *MIDGARD*.

DAMN ME FOR A FOOL FOR EVER CREATING THIS REALM. PLACE HAS BEEN NOTHING BUT TROUBLE.

AND *AYE*, PRETTY BIRD, I SAW IT FALL. 'TWAS *MJOLNIR* AND THE *ODIN-FORCE* THAT FINALLY FELLED THE *BASTARD*.

IT'S *STIRRING*. I HIT IT WITH BLASTS THAT WOULD MELT A SUPERNOVA, AND THE THING IS STILL MOVING.

NOT FOR LONG.

HHRRRRRGGH!!!

WELL, *THAT* TOOK SOME CONSIDERABLE EFFORT.

STILL YOUR FLAMING TONGUE.

WHERE ARE THE OTHERS? DID ANY SURVIVE?

HERE.

TAP TAP

HEY. WAKE UP IN THERE.

LIKE I SAID, THESE ARE THE QUESTIONS THAT KEEP ME AWAKE AT NIGHT.

I GUESS I DON'T MIND NOT SLEEPING. I MEAN, I CAN ALWAYS FIND A WAY TO FILL MORE HOURS IN THE DAY. BUT I DO MISS THE *DREAMS*.

WAAHHH.

DREAMED... I WAS RIDING... A *MASTODON*. AND THERE WAS AN *IRON FIST* AND A *BLACK PANTHER* AND...

OVER HERE, KID.

I USED TO HAVE SOME PRETTY WONDERFUL DREAMS.

I WONDER WHEN I STOPPED.

I'M GOING TO NEED YOU TO STEP OUT OF THE CAR.

AND WHY IT TOOK SO LONG FOR ME TO NOTICE.

UH. WHERE... THE HELL *AM* I?

LAST THING I REMEMBER, I WAS HOME, WORKING ON THE CAR. MUST'VE DOZED OFF AND...

THIS... THIS DOESN'T LOOK LIKE *EAST L.A.*

ALL RIGHT, *OUT.* LAST WARNING.

"...I'M HERE TO SAVE THE WORLD."

GOOD OF YOU BOYS TO FINALLY DROP IN.

BLAME TRAVIS HERE FOR OUR BEING LATE. HE WAS CONVINCED WE WERE BEING FOLLOWED.

I'M TELLING YOU, THE SAME TRUCK WAS BEHIND US FOR MILES. A BEER TRUCK, OF ALL THE--

CAN WE JUST GET THIS OVER WITH? SOME OF US HAVE TO GET BUSY BEING, YOU KNOW, UNEMPLOYED.

YEAH, CAN'T BELIEVE THIS IS HAPPENING TO YOU GUYS, THAT THEY'RE SHUTTING DOWN THE WHOLE SHEBANG. I MEAN, S.H.I.E.L.D. ALWAYS SEEMED LIKE SUCH A STABLE ORGANIZATION.

YOU BOYS MUST BE FROM THE PENTAGON'S WISEASS DEPARTMENT, HUH? WELL BELIEVE ME, IN THIS ROOM, THERE'S NOTHING TO LAUGH ABOUT.

YOU'RE LOOKING AT S.H.I.E.L.D.'S DEEPEST, DARKEST, MOST DANGEROUS LITTLE SECRETS. ANY ONE OF THESE CRATES COULD BLOW YOU ALL TO HELL A THOUSAND TIMES OVER. SO ENJOY THE LONG, BUMPY RIDE BACK TO AREA 51, FELLAS.

TERRIFIC. YOU GOT SOME SORT OF MANIFEST FOR ALL THIS DIRTY LAUNDRY? PLEASE TELL ME IT'S ALL IN ORDER.

IT IS. WELL, ALMOST.

ALL EXCEPT FOR THIS.

THERE'S NO RECORD OF THIS CRATE ANYWHERE. NO IDEA WHERE IT CAME FROM OR HOW LONG IT'S BEEN HERE.

ANY CLUE WHAT'S IN IT?

IF YOU'RE DUMB ENOUGH TO OPEN IT AND FIND OUT, BE MY GUEST.

GUYS, IS IT JUST ME OR IS IT FREEZING COLD IN HERE ALL OF A...

4-1939

AAAAARRRGGGH!!!

BIG ANGRY SNOWMEN! NO, THIS IS NOT A JOKE! SEND *BACKUP*! SEND *ALL* THE BACKUP!

HOLY HELL. GOOD THING WE BROUGHT YOU TWO.

THEY'RE ON SUBLEVEL NINE. ELEVATORS ARE OVER...

WE WILL NOT REQUIRE ELEVATORS.

SECONDS LATER.
SUBLEVEL NINE.

KROOOM

FROST GIANTS. SMALL ONES.

THEY DON'T LOOK SO SMALL TO ME.

THEY WILL ONCE WE ARE FINISHED WITH THEM.

GUESS I CAN GIVE THE OLD THREADS SOME ACTION THIS ONE LAST TIME.

IF THIS IS TRULY THE END OF YOUR TIME AS THE CAPTAIN, THEN LET US MAKE THE MOST OF THIS DAY.

KILL THE THOR WOM--

GAGGH!

As *JANE FOSTER*, she might be losing her battle with cancer, but no one said you couldn't have fun while dying.

Which is why *THOR* will definitely be *MAKING OUT* with *CAPTAIN AMERICA* today.

THERE WILL BE THE SWEET TASTE OF COMBAT, THEN OF MEAD.

THEN PERHAPS OF YOUR *LIPS*.

KISSING CAN WAIT. FOR NOW LET'S STICK TO THE PUNCHING.

YOU GUYS GET BEHIND ME.

YES, SIR.

SAM WILSON will miss the salutes, but with the real Steve Rogers finally back, Sam's ready to let go of the shield and be his own man again.

MAYBE AFTER JUST A FEW MORE SWINGS.

ENOUGH!

WELL, LOOK WHAT YOU JUST UNCOVERED, BIG GUY. MUST BE AN OLD PROTOTYPE SHIELD OR--

LAY DOWN YOUR WEAPONS! OR I TEAR THROUGH THIS MEAT-SACK LIKE A SNOWNADO FULL OF RAZOR SLEET!

NOW, YOU BLITHERING...

GAGGH.

LOOKS LIKE THE BACKUP FOR THE BACKUP JUST ARRIVED.

HEY, SORRY I'M TARDY. GOT A BIT LOST IN SOME...LET'S JUST CALL IT "SUPER SCIENCE" AND MOVE ON.

THOR, MEET *IRONHEART*. IRONHEART, MEET THE FROST GIANTS.

YEAH, WE JUST MET. THOUGH I'M HAPPY TO MEET A FEW MORE.

IF BY MEET, YOU MEAN *BLUDGEON*, THEN AYE, LADY OF IRON, THOR CONCURS.

RIGHT. BLUDGEONING IT IS.

"IN OTHER NEWS, THE NATIONWIDE MANHUNT CONTINUES FOR THE COSTUMED ASSASSIN KNOWN AS DEADPOOL, BUSINESSMAN WILSON FISK PULLS AHEAD IN THE LATEST NEW YORK MAYORAL POLLS, AND THE WHOLE COUNTRY IS STILL ASKING...

4-1939

"...WHERE IS CAPTAIN AMERICA?"

AFTER THE RECENT **HYDRA** TAKEOVER OF THE COUNTRY...IT'S STILL WEIRD TO SAY THAT OUT LOUD, ISN'T IT?

BUT AFTER EVERYTHING HIS SUPPOSED "DOPPELGANGER" PUT THIS COUNTRY THROUGH, WE ALL WANT TO KNOW... WHERE IS THE **REAL STEVE ROGERS** HIDING?

NO Large bills

AND WHEN WILL HE **ANSWER** FOR WHAT'S BEEN DONE IN HIS NAME?

ANOTHER CUP?

PROBABLY A GOOD IDEA.

THAT'S YOUR **BIKE** OUT FRONT, RIGHT? LONG DRIVE AHEAD OF YA?

I EXPECT SO.

WELL, WHERE YA **HEADED**, HANDSOME?

WISH I KNEW, MA'AM.

YOU'RE WATCHING **ROXX NEWS.** AND NOW A WORD FROM YOUR FRIENDS AT THE ROXXON ENERGY CORPORATION.

MIND IF WE TURN OFF THAT TV?

STEVE ROGERS ISN'T SLEEPING MUCH EITHER THESE DAYS. LIKE ME, HIS THOUGHTS ARE OF LEGACIES. HOW EASILY THEY SLIP AWAY...

"THIS HAD BETTER BE GOOD."

STARK FACILITY.
DOVER, NEW JERSEY.

AND I MEAN LIKE *THE WIRE SEASON 4* KINDA GOOD. I'VE ONLY GOT ABOUT 5,000 THINGS I NEED TO BE DOING RIGHT NOW.

YES, *MS. WATSON.* WE JUST COULDN'T SAY ANYTHING ABOUT THE PROBLEM OUTSIDE OF THE RESTRICTED AREA. IT'S, UH, IT'S ABOUT...

WELL, YOU SHOULD JUST SEE FOR YOURSELF.

IS THIS SOME KIND OF JOKE? I'M LOOKING AT *NOTHING.*

YES, MA'AM, THAT'S THE PROBLEM. HE WAS STILL HERE AN HOUR AGO, AT LEAST ACCORDING TO THE SURVEILLANCE CAMERAS.

AND THEN, JUST GONE.

YOU'RE TELLING ME...

I'M TELLING YOU THERE WERE NO FLUCTUATIONS IN HIS BIOSIGNS. NO TRACE OF ANYONE OR ANYTHING ELSE ENTERING THE ROOM.

A MAN IN A *COMA* DOESN'T JUST GET UP AND WALK AWAY, SO SOMEBODY, ANYBODY, PLEASE TELL ME...

WHERE THE HELL IS TONY STARK?

EVEN IN A WORLD THAT'S ALWAYS CHANGING.

SO DOES THIS MEAN WE'RE, LIKE...THE AVENGERS NOW?

BECAUSE THE THREE OF US TOGETHER, I DON'T KNOW...IT FEELS KIND OF AVENGERY.

RIGHT?

CALL US WHATEVER YOU LIKE-- AFTER WE'VE FINISHED WITH THE BLOODTHIRSTY MONSTERS WHO ARE TRYING TO MURDER US.

LET HER SAY IT.

WHAT?

I WILL NOT DIE FIGHTING FROST GIANTS. NOT TODAY. BUT NONE OF US KNOWS WHAT THE MORROW WILL BRING. HOW LONG WE'VE GOT TO CARRY THESE MANTLES.

OR HOW LONG TO *LIVE*.

EACH MOMENT IS SO PRECIOUS. SO LET HER SAY IT, IF SHE LIKES.

OKAY. BE MY GUEST, RIRI.

YOU MEAN... *WOW.* OKAY.

AVENGERS...

WAIT, WHAT'S THE LINE?

AAAND SO THE MOMENT PASSES.

'TWAS NEVER MY FAVORITE RALLYING CRY ANYWAY. I PREFER SOMETHING ABOUT *SMITING.*

SOMETIMES SO LOST, PEOPLE FORGET WE EVER EXISTED.

BENHAZIN STAR SYSTEM.

THE PLANET OF BAST.

BIRNIN T'CHALLA, THRONEWORLD OF...

...THE INTERGALACTIC EMPIRE OF WAKANDA.

THAT'S THE LAST OF THEM

THOSE BONDS WILL HOLD?

ACCORDING TO S.H.I.E.L.D., THEY WERE MADE TO RESTRAIN THE HULK.

THOUGH NOW THAT I THINK OF IT, THAT NEVER REALLY WORKED OUT SO WELL, DID IT?

THE TECH'S KIND OF ANTIQUATED. VERY 2015. I COULD MAKE A FEW ADJUSTMENTS, IF YOU LIKE.

THANK YOU.

CAP, THOR AND, UM, IRON MA'AM.

IRONHEART.

THANK YOU. ALL OF YOU. WE... WE LOST SOME GOOD MEN TODAY, BUT WE'D ALL HAVE BEEN DEAD IF IT WEREN'T FOR YOU THREE.

ANY IDEA WHAT THEY WERE AFTER DOWN HERE? OR IF THEY FOUND IT?

GIVE MJOLNIR AND I A MOMENT ALONE WITH ONE OF THEM, AND WE SHALL FIND OUT.

WE'RE SWEEPING NOW, BUT SO FAR, EVERYTHING SEEMS TO BE ACCOUNTED FOR...

RRRRRRRRGGH!

YOU STUPID WARM-BLOODED WORM! I WILL GRIND YOU INTO GRISTLE!

STOP HIDING AND GET OUT HERE! YOU HEAR ME IN THERE?!

SURE DO.

SHE TELLS HERSELF SHE'S COME HERE TO THE REMOTE WILDS OF CANADA IN ORDER TO VISIT THE GRAVE OF A FELLOW X-MAN.

BUT DEEP DOWN, *JEAN GREY* KNOWS THAT ISN'T WHAT SHE'S GOING TO FIND.

JEAN KNOWS BETTER THAN ANYONE THAT SOMETIMES THE DEAD CAN RISE FROM THE ASHES. REMADE. REBORN. RENEWED.

THAT IS HER LEGACY. HER PAST AND HER FUTURE.

HEH.

AND NOW...

...IT'S *HIS,* TOO.

WELCOME BACK.

WE MISSED YOU.

HEROES RISE AND FALL. THAT HAS ALWAYS BEEN THE WAY OF OUR LIVES.

CATACLYSM LOOMS AND THEN IS AVERTED AT THE LAST POSSIBLE MOMENT, UNTIL THE NEXT ONE COMES ALONG.

BUT THIS MOMENT FEELS DIFFERENT.

NEVER HAS IT BEEN LOOMING QUITE THIS CLOSE, IN SO MANY DIFFERENT WAYS. NEVER HAVE WE FELT SO INCAPABLE OF FACING IT.

SO VERY MUCH NOT OURSELVES.

SO VERY LOST.

SO WHAT DO WE DO?

I SUPPOSE WE DO WHAT OUR KIND HAS ALWAYS DONE.

WHAT HAS BECOME OUR *LEGACY.*

WE STAND ON THE SHOULDERS OF SUPER GENIUSES AND SPACE GODS, CLOSE OUR EYES AND IMAGINE A BETTER, BRIGHTER, MORE AMAZING TOMORROW.

THEN BRING IT TO LIFE.

SOMETHING GRAND AND FUN AND MIND-STAGGERINGLY RIDICULOUS. SOMETHING FULL OF HOPE AND COMPASSION.

SOMETHING BOTH REAL AND PROFOUNDLY UNREAL. SOMETHING MAD. SOMETHING MAGICAL.

SOMETHING *FANTAS--*

WHAT ARE YOU DOING?

MARVEL LEGACY #1 VARIANT BY **GREG LAND & FRANK D'ARMATA**

MARVEL IS PROUD TO PRESENT MARVEL PRIMER PAGES, THREE ALL-NEW PAGES OF COMIC CONTENT WRITTEN BY ROBBIE THOMPSON (*SILK, DOCTOR STRANGE AND THE SORCERERS SUPREME*) WITH A MAJORITY OF ART FROM ACCLAIMED SUPERSTAR MARK BAGLEY (*AMAZING SPIDER-MAN, ALL-NEW X-MEN, ULTIMATE SPIDER-MAN*). THESE STORIES WILL DRAW READERS INTO THE MARVEL UNIVERSE LIKE NEVER BEFORE. EACH STORY PROVIDES EASY ACCESS INTO THE WORLD OF EACH TITLE CHARACTER, AS WELL AS INTO THE LEGACY STORIES. DESIGNED TO GIVE NEW READERS A HOOK INTO THE SERIES, MARVEL PRIMER PAGES WILL OFFER FANS A SIMPLE JUMPING-ON POINT FOR ALMOST ALL OF MARVEL'S HEROIC AND ICONIC CHARACTERS.

"WHEN I FIRST APPROACHED ROBBIE AND MARK TO DO THESE PRIMER STORIES, I GAVE THEM ONLY ONE EDICT: TO REMIND ALL READERS BOTH WHO THESE CHARACTERS ARE AND WHAT THEY'RE ABOUT IN THREE ALL-NEW PAGES," SAID MARVEL EDITOR DARREN SHAN. "WHAT WE GOT BACK HAS BEEN SOME OF THE MOST FUN ART I'VE EVER SEEN FROM MARK! AND WE COULDN'T BE LUCKIER TO HAVE SOMEONE LIKE ROBBIE TO CHERRY-PICK THE MOST CLASSIC MOMENTS IN MARVEL HISTORY. THEN THE TWO OF THEM TIE THIS ALL UP INTO ONE PERFECT PACKAGE. I THINK EVERYONE WILL LOVE THESE!"

"IT'S BEEN AN ABSOLUTE BLAST WORKING ON THIS PROJECT — IT GIVES ME A GREAT EXCUSE TO RE-READ SO MANY OF MY FAVORITE COMICS!" THOMPSON SAID. I'VE BEEN A FAN OF MARK'S FOR YEARS, SO TO GET TO WORK WITH HIM IS A DREAM COME TRUE. MARK TAKES THE SCRIPTS AND DISTILLS THEM DOWN TO THEIR ESSENCE, FINDING BRILLIANT WAYS TO TELL THESE STORIES WITH TRULY ICONIC IMAGES. I CAN'T WAIT FOR PEOPLE TO SEE WHAT HE'S DONE WITH THESE!"

"THIS LEGACY GIG HAS BEEN A LOT OF FUN TO WORK ON AND A BIT OF AN EDUCATION...EVEN FOR SOMEONE WHO HAS BEEN DRAWING COMICS FOR AS LONG AS I HAVE! I THINK READERS WILL REALLY ENJOY THE STORIES WE'RE REVISITING," BAGLEY ADDED.

MARVEL PRIMER PAGES GIVE EVERY FAN THE OPPORTUNITY TO TRULY "MAKE MINE MARVEL" BY PROVIDING THE MOST ACCESSIBLE WAY TO ENJOY MARVEL COMICS — ENSURING THAT LONGTIME FANS WILL FALL IN LOVE WITH THEIR FAVORITE STORIES ALL OVER AGAIN, AND THAT NEW FANS WILL BE DRAWN INTO MARVEL'S MAGICAL UNIVERSE OF ADVENTURE AND HEROICS.

THERE ARE A BILLION DIMENSIONS IN THE MULTIVERSE. BUT I AM FROM A *SINGULAR* DIMENSION.

THE UTOPIAN PARALLEL.

WHICH MY *MOMS* SAID MADE ME ONE OF A KIND.

WE LIVED IN THE PRESENCE OF THE *DEMIURGE,* A SENTIENT LIFE FORCE THAT GAVE MY FAMILY *POWERS...*

...POWERS MY PARENTS USED TO *SAVE* THE UTOPIAN PARALLEL FROM BEING *CONSUMED* BY BLACK HOLES.

THEY DIED, SO THAT *WE* COULD LIVE.

THEY WERE *HEROES.*

I WAS BOUND AND DETERMINED TO *FOLLOW* THEIR EXAMPLE.

I LEFT THE COMFORTS OF HOME, HOPPING FROM ONE DIMENSION TO THE NEXT, UNTIL I FOUND...

...EARTH.

MY NEW HOME.

I JOINED THE TEEN BRIGADE...

...THEN FOUGHT ALONGSIDE THE *YOUNG AVENGERS.*

EVENTUALLY, I *LED* THE ULTIMATES.

BUT WHEN YOU'RE ONE OF A KIND...

ROBBIE THOMPSON: writer   DAVID LOPEZ: artist   JOSÉ VILLARRUBIA: colorist
TRAVIS LANHAM: letterer   KATHLEEN WISNESKI: assistant editor   DARREN SHAN: editor

TRUTH BE TOLD, I SHOULDN'T EXIST.

I WAS CREATED IN A LAB BY DR. SARAH KINNEY.

THE GENETIC CLONE OF ONE OF THE GREATEST MUTANTS EVER. LOGAN. THE *WOLVERINE.*

DR. KINNEY CARRIED ME TO TERM. BROUGHT ME INTO THIS WORLD...

...WHERE I WAS TRAINED TO BE A *KILLER.*

MONSTERS LIKE DR. ZANDER RICE *ACCELERATED* MY TRAINING.

I WAS AN ASSASSIN FOR HIRE.

A *WEAPON.*

THERE WERE MANY CLONES...

THEY CALLED ME X-23.

WHEN I FAILED TO KILL A SMALL CHILD, THOUGH, DR. KINNEY DIDN'T SEE ME AS A KILLER ANYMORE. SHE SAW SOMETHING NO ONE ELSE SAW...

ROBBIE THOMPSON
WRITER

MARK BAGLEY
PENCILER

ANDREW HENNESSY
INKER

DAN BROWN
COLORIST

VC'S CORY PETIT
LETTERER

KATHLEEN WISNESKI
ASSISTANT EDITOR

DARREN SHAN
EDITOR

the AMAZING SPIDER-MAN

I TRIED TO KEEP THINGS SIMPLE.

YOU CAN SEE HOW THAT'S WORKED FOR ME SO FAR.

I'LL SAY THIS MUCH...

...IT'S NEVER BORING.

AND THE BEST PART?

ROBBIE THOMPSON
WRITER

MARK BAGLEY
PENCILER

JOHN DELL
INKER

DAN BROWN
COLORIST

VC'S JOE CARAMAGNA
LETTERER

KATHLEEN WISNESKI
ASSISTANT EDITOR

DARREN SHAN
EDITOR

MY NAME IS PETER PARKER.

WHEN I WAS A TEENAGER, I THOUGHT MY LIFE HAD CHANGED FOREVER AFTER I WAS BITTEN BY A RADIOACTIVE SPIDER.

THAT SPIDER BITE GAVE ME *POWERS*, WHICH I USED TO BECOME...

...the AMAZING SPIDER-MAN

BEING SPIDER-MAN WAS AWESOME. BUT MY LIFE REALLY CHANGED...

FACE IT, TIGER, YOU JUST HIT THE JACKPOT!

...WHEN I MET *MARY JANE WATSON*.

AND LIKE ALWAYS-- SHE WAS RIGHT. I *DID* HIT THE JACKPOT.

MARY JANE IS THE KINDEST, FUNNIEST, MOST INCREDIBLE PERSON I KNOW. AND FOR REASONS I'LL NEVER UNDERSTAND, BUT I'M ETERNALLY GRATEFUL FOR...

...SHE *MARRIED* MJ.

WITH MJ, I LEARNED WHAT THE *GREATEST* RESPONSIBILITY CAN BE...

...WHEN *ANNIE MAY PARKER* CAME INTO OUR LIVES.

SUDDENLY THE WHOLE WORLD WAS JUST MY FAMILY.

I WAS SPIDER-MAN NO MORE.

BUT NOT FOR LONG. BECAUSE, MY KID?

SHE'S A CHIP OFF THE OLD BLOCK.

AND MY WIFE?

WELL, MJ'S ALWAYS BEEN A ROCK STAR.

MY FAMILY IS *STILL* MY WORLD, BUT NOW, *TOGETHER*...

...THE XAVIER INSTITUTE FOR HIGHER LEARNING.

CHARLES BROUGHT MUTANTS FROM ALL OVER THE WORLD TO HIS HOME, WHERE HE TAUGHT THEM TO CONTROL THEIR POWERS.

HE BECAME PROFESSOR X, WHILE HIS FIRST STUDENTS BECAME...

X-MEN

...A GROUP OF MUTANTS PROTECTING A WORLD THAT FEARS AND HATES THEM.

OVER THE YEARS, MANY VERSIONS OF THE TEAM WERE FORMED AND DISBANDED.

IN THE END, CHARLES' DREAM OF PEACEFUL COEXISTENCE...

...COST HIM HIS LIFE... AT THE HANDS OF HIS VERY FIRST STUDENT, CYCLOPS.

BUT CHARLES HAS DIED BEFORE. AND HE SHALL RETURN AGAIN WITH THE HELP OF HIS FELLOW MUTANTS...

ROBBIE THOMPSON WRITER CARLOS PACHECO PENCILER RAFAEL FONTERIZ INKER EDGAR DELGADO COLORIST
VC'S CLAYTON COWLES LETTERER KATHLEEN WISNESKI ASST. EDITOR DARREN SHAN EDITOR

IT ALL STARTED WITH A TRICK.

OR RATHER, A *TRICKSTER*.

THE ASGARDIAN GOD LOKI ENACTED A PLAN OF REVENGE AGAINST HIS BROTHER THOR FOR EXILING HIM TO THE ISLE OF SILENCE.

HE *TRICKED* PEOPLE INTO BELIEVING THE HULK CAUSED A DISASTER, KNOWING THE HEROIC THOR WOULD BE CALLED INTO BATTLE AGAINST THE GREEN MENACE...

...AND MOST CERTAINLY DEFEATED.

BUT LOKI'S TRICK SOON TURNED ON HIM...

HULK ATTACKS TRAIN

CITY NEWS

...AS HIS ACTIONS INADVERTENTLY BROUGHT EARTH'S MIGHTIEST HEROES *TOGETHER* FOR THE FIRST TIME.

THEY UNITED AS ONE TO DEFEAT A COMMON ENEMY. AND WHEN THEY DISCOVERED THAT *LOKI* WAS BEHIND THIS...

THE AVENGERS WERE BORN!

THROUGHOUT THE YEARS, THERE HAVE BEEN MANY MEMBERS...

...WHO FOUGHT MANY VILLAINS...

...ALL OF THEM UNITED WITH A SIMPLE BATTLE CRY...

ROBBIE THOMPSON
WRITER

DANIEL ACUÑA
ARTIST

VC'S CORY PETIT
LETTERER

KATHLEEN WISNESKI
ASSISTANT EDITOR

DARREN SHAN
EDITOR

...T'CHAKA, MY *FATHER.*

AS KING AND BLACK PANTHER, MY FATHER MADE WAKANDA THE GREATEST AND MOST TECHNOLOGICALLY ADVANCED COUNTRY IN HISTORY.

HE KEPT US *HIDDEN* FROM THE WORLD. IT WAS A PEACEFUL TIME. A HAPPY TIME...

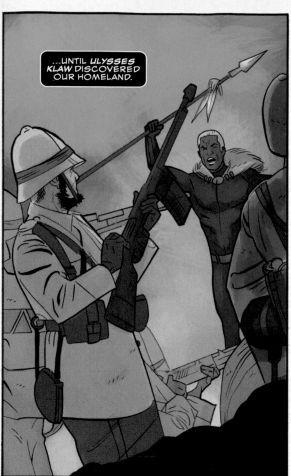

...UNTIL *ULYSSES KLAW* DISCOVERED OUR HOMELAND.

IN HIS RUTHLESS PURSUIT OF VIBRANIUM, HE TOOK MY FATHER'S LIFE.

I *AVENGED* MY FATHER'S DEATH, AND BROUGHT KLAW TO HEEL.

AND IN THAT MOMENT, THE MANTLE WAS PASSED TO ME.

MY NAME IS T'CHALLA...

ZAK

...THE **BLACK PANTHER**

ROBBIE THOMPSON WRITER
WILFREDO TORRES ARTIST
DAN BROWN COLORIST
VC'S JOE SABINO LETTERER
KATHLEEN WISNESKI ASSISTANT EDITOR
DARREN SHAN EDITOR

OF COURSE, HIS REAL NAME IS BLACKAGAR BOLTAGON.

THE CHILD OF TWO OF ATTILAN'S TOP MINDS.

THE CHILD OF ATTILAN'S KING AND QUEEN.

HE WAS EXPOSED TO *TERRIGEN* BEFORE HE WAS BORN. AND AS RESULT...

...HE WAS GIVEN POWERS BEYOND EXPECTATION. COSMIC AWARENESS AND ENERGY-MANIPULATING ABILITIES THAT MANIFESTED IN HIS *VOICE*.

EVEN A *WHISPER* HELD DESTRUCTIVE POWER.

HE WAS KEPT IN A SOUNDPROOF ROOM, WHERE HIS FATHER TAUGHT HIM TO CONTROL HIS ABILITIES.

HE HELD HIS POWER IN CHECK UNTIL HIS SCHEMING BROTHER, *MAXIMUS*, WORKING ALONGSIDE THE KREE, HATCHED A PLAN TO UPEND LIFE IN ATTILAN.

BLACKAGAR USED HIS POWERS TO SAVE HIS HOME, BUT THE SHIP HE DESTROYED CRASHED INTO THE CITY, KILLING HIS PARENTS, RESULTING IN BLACKAGAR BECOMING...

...KING OF THE INHUMANS.

FOR YEARS, THE SILENT KING KEPT THE PEACE.

AND HIS SILENCE.

UNTIL...

...HIS VOICE DETONATED THE TERRIGEN BOMB, DEFEATING THANOS, BUT DESTROYING ATTILAN IN THE PROCESS. HIS KINGDOM WAS GONE...

...BUT THE TERRIGEN MIST SPREAD OVER EARTH, CREATING A NEW GENERATION OF INHUMANS. A NEW GENERATION OF HEROES.

AND THEN, THE KING WITHOUT A THRONE BECAME...

...A PRISONER.

MAXIMUS HAD LONG SOUGHT REVENGE AGAINST HIS BROTHER.

FACING IMPRISONMENT FOR HIS MYRIAD CRIMES, HE FINALLY HAD HIS CHANCE.

MAXIMUS USED HIS PSYCHIC ABILITIES TO HAVE BLACKAGAR SENT IN HIS PLACE.

BLACKAGAR EVENTUALLY WON BACK HIS FREEDOM, AND NOW HE SEEKS TO HELP HIS PEOPLE.

FOR WHETHER HE LIKES IT OR NOT, HE IS KING OF THE INHUMANS.

HE IS...

MILES WARREN.

A.K.A. THE JACKAL.

USING STOLEN GENETIC MATERIAL, WARREN CREATED A CLONE OF HIS NEMESIS...

...PETER PARKER.

A.K.A. SPIDER-MAN.

THE JACKAL WANTED THE CLONE TO DESTROY SPIDER-MAN ONCE AND FOR ALL.

BUT THE CLONE WAS BORN WITH PETER'S MEMORIES AS WELL. THE CLONE BELIEVED HE WAS PETER PARKER.

AFTER BEING PRESUMED DEAD, THE CLONE WAS REBORN, ONLY TO REALIZE HE WAS A CLONE AFTER ALL.

HE LEFT THE TOWN HE BELIEVED TO BE HIS HOME IN EXILE.

HE TOOK TWO FAMILY NAMES AND BECAME...

...BEN REILLY.

BEN WANDERED IN SEARCH OF MEANING.

BUT NO MATTER WHERE HE WENT, NO MATTER WHAT HE DID, HE WAS DRAWN BACK TO NEW YORK.

BACK TO SPIDER-MAN.

IT COST HIM HIS LIFE.

HE WAS RESURRECTED BY MILES WARREN.

AGAIN. AND AGAIN. AND AGAIN.

BUT EVEN IN DEATH, THERE WAS NO PEACE FOR BEN.

UNTIL BEN FINALLY TURNED THE TABLES ON HIS CREATOR...

...AND *BECAME* THE JACKAL.

HE POSSESSED GREAT POWER BUT TOOK NO *RESPONSIBILITY*.

HIS MIND NOW SPLIT BETWEEN THE BEN AND THE JACKAL PERSONAS, BEN BATTLES HIS INNER DEMONS, SEEKING TO FIND THE *MEANING* OF HIS LIFE, SEEKING OUT HIS REDEMPTION AS...

BEN REILLY:
THE SCARLET SPIDER

ROBBIE THOMPSON
WRITER

TODD NAUCK
ARTIST

RACHELLE ROSENBERG
COLORIST

VC'S JOE CARAMAGNA
LETTERER

KATHLEEN WISNESKI
ASSISTANT EDITOR

DARREN SHAN
EDITOR

APOCALYPSE LEARNED OF MISTER SINISTER'S PLAN AND *INFECTED* ME WITH A DEADLY TECHNO-ORGANIC VIRUS.

MY FATHER WAS GIVEN AN IMPOSSIBLE CHOICE--SEND ME TO THE DISTANT FUTURE FOR A *CHANCE* AT A CURE...

...OR WATCH ME DIE.

HE SENT ME TO THE FUTURE.

WHERE THE IMPOSSIBLE WAS *POSSIBLE.*

THE PSYCHES OF SCOTT AND JEAN GREY-SUMMERS WERE BROUGHT *FORWARD* IN TIME WITH ME AND *INTO* SLYM AND REDD DAYSPRING. THEY *RAISED* ME...

...*TRAINED* ME TO USE MY MUTANT POWERS TO KEEP THE *VIRUS* AT BAY. I WAS MY OWN CURE. AND IN TIME, I BECAME...

...CABLE!

NOW I TRAVEL *THROUGH* TIME TO SAVE MUTANTS AND HUMANS ALIKE. I AM THE LINK TO THE...

...PAST...

...PRESENT...

...AND *FUTURE.*

ROBBIE THOMPSON: WRITER **MARK BAGLEY:** PENCILER **JOHN DELL:** INKER
ANDY TROY: COLORS **VC'S TRAVIS LANHAM:** LETTERING
KATHLEEN WISNESKI: ASSISTANT EDITOR **DARREN SHAN:** EDITOR

WHEN I FINALLY GOT OUT OF PRISON, I DECIDED TO USE MY NEWFOUND POWERS TO DO *GOOD* IN THE WORLD...

...TO GIVE BACK.

I BECAME A HERO FOR HIRE...

...EVEN AN *AVENGER.*

BUT NO MATTER WHERE I WENT...

...I *NEVER* FORGOT WHERE I CAME FROM.

I JUST DON'T UNDERSTAND THE FASHION OF TODAY'S YOUTH. FIND YOURSELF A DECENT SHIRT.

YES, MA'AM.

ROBBIE THOMPSON WRITER MARK BAGLEY PENCILER JOHN DELL INKER ISRAEL SILVA COLORIST
VC'S JOE SABINO LETTERER KATHLEEN WISNESKI ASSISTANT EDITOR DARREN SHAN EDITOR

NOW, STEVE ROGERS IS A MAN OUT OF TIME, BUT HE STILL FIGHTS FOR WHAT IS RIGHT, BECAUSE HE WILL ALWAYS BE...

CAPTAIN AMERICA

ROBBIE THOMPSON
WRITER

VALERIO SCHITI
ARTIST

FRANK D'ARMATA
COLORIST

VC'S JOE CARAMAGNA
LETTERER

KATHLEEN WISNESKI
ASSISTANT EDITOR

DARREN SHAN
EDITOR

...CAPTAIN MARVEL

I FIGHT TO KEEP EARTH SAFE--AS AN AVENGER, AND NOW AS THE LEADER OF ALPHA FLIGHT.

AND ALONG THE WAY I *FINALLY* FOUND WHERE I BELONG...

...AMONG THE STARS.

ROBBIE THOMPSON
WRITER

BRENT SCHOONOVER
ARTIST

JORDAN BOYD
COLORIST

VC'S JOE CARAMAGNA
LETTERER

KATHLEEN WISNESKI
ASSISTANT EDITOR

DARREN SHAN
EDITOR

WE HAVE ONE MISSION.

CHANGE THE WORLD.

SIMPLE, RIGHT? WE DIDN'T THINK SO, EITHER, SO WE RECRUITED...

...AMADEUS CHO, WHOM YOU PROBABLY KNOW AS THE **TOTALLY AWESOME HULK**...

...THEN VIV, A TEENAGED SYNTHEZOID WHO WAS CREATED BY THE VISION. YEAH, **THE** VISION.

AND NO TEAM WOULD BE COMPLETE WITHOUT A TEENAGED SCOTT SUMMERS WHO TIME-TRAVELED TO THE PRESENT AND GOT STUCK HERE. Y'KNOW, **CYCLOPS.**

TOGETHER, WE'RE THE **NEXT** GENERATION OF HEROES. AND THIS NEXT GENERATION HAS TO BE **BETTER.** THEY HAVE TO BE...

...CHAMPIONS

ROBBIE THOMPSON WRITER
ALBERTO ALBURQUERQUE ARTIST
EMILIO LOPEZ COLORIST
VC'S CLAYTON COWLES LETTERER
KATHLEEN WISNESKI ASST. EDITOR
DARREN SHAN EDITOR

Gangsters *murdered* my father after he refused to throw a fight.

When the police failed to bring them to justice, I took matters into my own hands.

I trained with the help of *Stick*, a blind sensei who helped hone my special abilities.

Now, as a crime fighter, I bring the corrupt to justice...

...and as a lawyer, I make sure they stay where they belong.

My name is Matt Murdock, and I am...

...DAREDEVIL!

ROBBIE THOMPSON WRITER
ROD REIS ARTIST
VC'S CLAYTON COWLES LETTERER
KATHLEEN WISNESKI ASST. EDITOR
DARREN SHAN EDITOR

THE DEFENDERS

ROBBIE THOMPSON
WRITER

PERE PÉREZ
ARTIST

RUTH REDMOND
COLOR ARTIST

VC'S CORY PETIT
LETTERER

KATHLEEN WISNESKI
ASSISTANT EDITOR

DARREN SHAN
EDITOR

MY NAME IS *DOCTOR STEPHEN STRANGE.*

WHEN I BEGAN MY CAREER AS A NEUROSURGEON, I WANTED TO SAVE PEOPLE FOR THE RIGHT REASONS.

BUT YOUTHFUL ARROGANCE GOT IN THE WAY OF MY ALTRUISTIC GOALS. I SOUGHT MONEY, FAME AND FORTUNE. ALL OF IT LEADING ME DOWN A PATH...

...THAT NEARLY KILLED ME.

35 MPH

SEVERE NERVE DAMAGE *RUINED* MY HANDS.

I SOUGHT ANSWERS TO MY PROBLEM FROM EVERY CORNER OF THE EARTH.

AND THEN I DISCOVERED A *NEW* PATH, A PATH THAT INVOLVED...

...MAGIC.

I HAD HEARD RUMORS OF THE MAN KNOWN AS *THE ANCIENT ONE*--A MYSTICAL ENTITY WITH GREAT POWER. I BELIEVED HE COULD *HEAL* MY HANDS. INSTEAD...

...HE HEALED MY *SOUL*.

AND HE CHANGED ME INTO...

...A SORCERER SUPREME!

NOW, I HAVE REPLACED MY MASTER, AND IT IS MY SOLEMN DUTY TO DEFEND THIS WORLD FROM THE MAGICAL *AND* MYSTIFYING.

I MAY NO LONGER PRACTICE MEDICINE, BUT I REMAIN...

ROBBIE THOMPSON
WRITER

NIKO HENRICHON
ARTIST

VC'S CORY PETIT
LETTERER

KATHLEEN WISNESKI
ASSISTANT EDITOR

DARREN SHAN
EDITOR

...I FINALLY TOOK *FLIGHT.*

CAPTAIN AMERICA TOOK ME UNDER HIS WING.

TRAINED ME.

MADE ME AN *AVENGER.*

AND WHEN HE COULDN'T CARRY THE SHIELD...

...I HELD IT HIGH FOR HIM.

NO MATTER HOW HIGH I'VE SOARED, I'VE ALWAYS KEPT MY FEET ON THE GROUND.

I ALWAYS HELP THOSE IN NEED...

...I ALWAYS *LISTEN* TO MY PARENTS. AND IN THEIR HONOR, I SHALL ALWAYS BE...

...THE FALCON

ROBBIE THOMPSON
WRITER

MARK BAGLEY
PENCILER

ANDREW HENNESSY
INKER

ISRAEL SILVA
COLORIST

VC's JOE CARAMAGNA
LETTERER

KATHLEEN WISNESKI
ASSISTANT EDITOR

DARREN SHAN
EDITOR

...THE GUARDIANS of the GALAXY

ROBBIE THOMPSON
WRITER

MARCUS TO
ARTIST

IAN HERRING
COLOR ARTIST

VC'S CORY PETIT
LETTERER

KATHLEEN WISNESKI
ASSISTANT EDITOR

DARREN SHAN
EDITOR

JUST WHEN EVERYTHING WAS GETTING INTERESTING, MY BROTHER TEDDY PULLED ME BACK TO OUR BORING OLD *REAL* WORLD.

BUT THAT WORLD? WELL...

...IT MIGHT BE A FAKE COMIC-BOOK WORLD, TOO.

LIKE I SAID... WEIRD.

I'VE SEEN THE *REAL MARVEL UNIVERSE.* AND I'M GETTING BACK THERE.

THAT, OR I'M LOSING MY MARBLES. TOUGH CALL.

WHY DON'T YOU PICK UP THE FIRST TRADE, CATCH UP, THEN PRE-ORDER THIS COMIC AND HELP ME FIGURE IT ALL OUT, OKAY? K'BYE!

ROBBIE THOMPSON WRITER
MARK BAGLEY PENCILER
JOHN DELL INKER
JOSÉ VILLARRUBIA COLORIST
VC'S CLAYTON COWLES LETTERER
KATHLEEN WISNESKI ASST. EDITOR
DARREN SHAN EDITOR

COME ON, YOU FOOL! WE'VE GOT TO REACH THE PROTECTIVE TRENCH BEFORE THE BOMB GOES OFF!

BRUCE BANNER.

BRILLIANT SCIENTIST.

HERO.

IN SAVING AN INNOCENT KID, BRUCE WAS EXPOSED TO GAMMA RADIATION. AND IN SO DOING, HE BECAME...

...THE HULK!

BRUCE WAS GIVEN ENORMOUS POWER. POWER HE COULDN'T CONTROL. IT WAS A *CURSE.*

AMADEUS CHO.

GENIUS OF ALL TRADES.

AND, UM, *KIND* OF A HERO.

LUCKILY FOR ME, WHEN I GOT INTO A JAM...

...BRUCE BANNER *SAVED* ME.

AND IN TIME...

...I *RETURNED* THE FAVOR.

YOU NEVER ASKED FOR THIS, BRUCE. YOU NEVER WANTED THIS.

MAYBE IT'S TIME TO GIVE IT UP TO SOMEONE WHO *DOES.*

BANNER ABSORBED TOO MUCH KIBER RADIATION. HIS MIND AND BODY WERE OVERLOADED. HE WOULDN'T BE ABLE TO CONTAIN IT FOR MUCH LONGER. AND SO...

...I TRANSFERRED HIS *POWERS* TO M

NOW, I'M TURNING THI *CURSE* INTO SOMETHING GOOD A

THE INCREDIBLE HULK

ROBBIE THOMPSON
WRITER

JOE BENNETT
PENCILER

BELARDINO BRABO
INKER

ANDY TROY
COLORS

VC'S CORY PETIT
LETTERER

KATHLEEN WISNESKI
ASSISTANT EDITOR

DARREN SHAN
EDITOR

...ICEMAN!

ROBBIE THOMPSON WRITER
EDGAR SALAZAR ARTIST
RACHELLE ROSENBERG COLOR ARTIST
VC'S JOE SABINO LETTERER
KATHLEEN WISNESKI ASSISTANT EDITOR
DARREN SHAN EDITOR

RIRI WILLIAMS. TEENAGED PRODIGY. M.I.T. GENIUS.

LIKE TONY STARK BEFORE HER, RIRI USED HER ADVANCED INTELLECT TO BUILD HER OWN ARMOR. WITH THIS SUIT...

...A NEW HERO WAS BORN!

WHEN TONY DISCOVERED RIRI AND HER INVENTION, HE FOUND A KINDRED SPIRIT AND TOOK HER UNDER HIS WING.

TONY CREATED AN ARTIFICIAL INTELLIGENCE THAT LOOKS, SOUNDS AND IS ALMOST AS SMART AS HE IS--THIS A.I. ASSISTS RIRI AS SHE CONTINUES HER JOURNEY AS...

...IRONHEART

ROBBIE THOMPSON WRITER
VALERIO SCHITI ARTIST
FRANK D'ARMATA COLOR ARTIST
VC'S CLAYTON COWLES LETTERER
KATHLEEN WISNESKI ASST. EDITOR
DARREN SHAN EDITOR

...AND MAYBE A WAY TO MAKE A LITTLE MONEY.

SO, I WAS A *HERO FOR HIRE* FOR A WHILE.

EVEN AN AVENGER.

AND NOW I'M A DEFENDER.

BUT MOST IMPORTANT, I FINALLY FOUND MY WAY. I'M FINALLY BACK ON THE PATH MY PARENTS SET ME ON ALL THOSE YEARS AGO...

ROBBIE THOMPSON: WRITER
MARK BAGLEY: PENCILER
JOHN DELL: INKER
RACHELLE ROSENBERG: COLORIST
TRAVIS LANHAM: LETTERER
KATHLEEN WISNESKI: ASST. EDITOR
DARREN SHAN: EDITOR

MY **MUTANT** POWERS FIRST MANIFESTED WHEN MY BEST FRIEND WAS HIT BY A CAR.

I TELEPATHICALLY **BONDED** TO HER IN HER **FINAL** MOMENTS. I ALMOST DIED AS WELL.

I SUPPOSE MY POWERS HAVE **ALWAYS** BEEN LINKED WITH **DEATH.**

THE PSYCHIC TRAUMA LEFT ME IN A **COMA.**

BUT **PROFESSOR CHARLES XAVIER** HELPED BRING ME BACK.

HE TOLD ME MY TELEPATHIC AND TELEKINETIC POWERS DIDN'T HAVE TO BE A DANGER. HE TOLD ME THAT, CHANNELED PROPERLY...

...MY POWERS COULD **SAVE** LIVES.

I JOINED THE **X-MEN,** PROFESSOR XAVIER'S GROUP OF MUTANTS, AND TRAINED TO MAKE THE WORLD A BETTER PLACE.

...THE PHOENIX FORCE *FINDS* ME.

WITH THE HELP OF THE HEROES WHO HAVE FACED THE PHOENIX FORCE, OR BEEN A PART OF IT, I'M TRAINING TO MAKE SURE I NEVER SUCCUMB TO IT.

MY NAME IS

JEAN GREY

AND I WILL DO WHATEVER IT TAKES TO STOP THE PHOENIX FORCE BEFORE IT HARMS ANOTHER SOUL.

ROBBIE THOMPSON WRITER
MARK BAGLEY PENCILER **ANDREW HENNESSY** INKER
CHRIS SOTOMAYOR COLORIST **VC's TRAVIS LANHAM** LETTERER
KATHLEEN WISNESKI ASST. EDITOR **DARREN SHAN** EDITOR

MY NAME IS JESSICA JONES. AND I KNOW ONE THING IS TRUE IN THIS WORLD...

...LIFE SUCKS.

DON'T BELIEVE ME?

TOLD YOU.

WHEN I WOKE UP FROM THE ACCIDENT, I FOUND OUT MY FAMILY WAS *GONE*.

AND ALL I GOT WAS A ONE-WAY TICKET TO AN ORPHANAGE.

HAZAR EXPERIM MATERI PROPERTY U.S. MILIT

BUT THEN I REALIZED I GOT SOMETHING ELSE FROM THE ACCIDENT.

THE *RADIOACTIVE* MATERIAL MY FAMILY CRASHED INTO GAVE ME SUPER-POWERS. AND *THEN*...

NO, I BELONGED *HERE.*

HERE I CAN DO GOOD ON MY *OWN* TERMS--AS A PRIVATE DETECTIVE WORKING OUT OF A RAT-INFESTED BUILDING TAKING ON CLIENTS WHO USUALLY NEVER END UP PAYING ME.

LOOK, IT WORKS FOR ME. DON'T JUDGE.

I EVEN FOUND A PARTNER-IN-CRIME AND GOT *MARRIED.* SUCCESSFUL BUSINESS (ISH), SUCCESSFUL MARRIAGE (ISH). YOU KNOW WHAT?

AT LONG LAST, MAYBE, JUST MAYBE--

NAH, LIFE STILL SUCKS.

LET'S BE HONEST, I'LL PROBABLY SCREW THIS UP, TOO.

BUT IN THE MEANTIME, IF *YOUR* LIFE SUCKS 'CAUSE YOU FOUND YOURSELF IN A JAM, GIVE OLD *ALIAS INVESTIGATIONS* A CALL.

MAYBE I'LL HELP YOU.

NO PROMISES, 'KAY?

ROBBIE THOMPSON
WRITER

MARK BAGLEY
PENCILER

ANDREW HENNESSY
INKER

RACHELLE ROSENBERG
COLORIST

VC'S CORY PETIT
LETTERER

KATHLEEN WISNESKI
ASSISTANT EDITOR

DARREN SHAN
EDITOR

REED RICHARDS.

SUE STORM.

JOHNNY STORM.

AND *ME*-- BEN GRIMM.

THESE PEOPLE? WELL, THEY'RE MY *FAMILY*.

WE GOT EXPOSED TO *COSMIC RAYS* ON OUR FIRST ADVENTURE TOGETHER.

I *WARNED* REED, BUT HE'S TOO SMART TO LISTEN TO A DUMMY LIKE ME, I GUESS.

WHEN WE CRASH-LANDED BACK ON EARTH, EVERYONE REALIZED THE COSMIC RAYS GAVE US *POWERS*.

REED GOT ALL *STRETCHY*.

SUE COULD TURN *INVISIBLE*.

JOHNNY COULD LIGHT HIMSELF ON *FIRE*.

AND ME? ME IT TURNED INTA *A PILE A ROCKS*.

AND SO TOGETHER, WE BECAME...

THE Fantastic Four

LIKE ALL FAMILIES, WE FOUGHT.

ON GOOD DAYS, IT WAS US AGAINST BAD GUYS. ON BAD DAYS, IT WAS US AGAINST EACH OTHER.

WE HAD MORE GOOD DAYS THAN BAD.

BUT NOTHING LASTS FOREVER.

JOHNNY EVENTUALLY WOUND UP WITH THE *INHUMANS*.

AND ME, WELL, I'M A PILOT, SO WHAT BETTER PLACE FOR ME THAN IN THE STARS WITH *THE GUARDIANS OF THE GALAXY?*

NO MATTER WHERE WE GO, THOUGH, OR WHAT WE'VE BEEN THROUGH... WE BELONG *TOGETHER*.

REED AND SUE ARE *GONE* NOW.

BUT JOHNNY AND I, WELL, WE'RE STILL...

MARVEL ② IN ONE

ROBBIE THOMPSON
WRITER

GREG LAND
PENCILER

JAY LEISTEN
INKER

FRANK D'ARMATA
COLORIST

VC'S JOE CARAMAGNA
LETTERER

KATHLEEN WISNESKI
ASSISTANT EDITOR

DARREN SHAN
EDITOR

...I was **wrong**. Devil Dinosaur and I **switch bodies** when the moon is full. Bad for him...

...even **worse** for me.

HELP!

UM, SORRY...? MY BAD!

We're still working out the kinks, to be honest.

But this...

...is my **life** now.

Hey, at least I've finally got a **friend**. And together, we're...

MOON GIRL AND DEVIL DINOSAUR

ROBBIE THOMPSON: writer
MARCO FAILLA: artist
MIKE SPICER: colorist
VC'S TRAVIS LANHAM: letterer
KATHLEEN WISNESKI: asst. editor
DARREN SHAN: editor

...UNTIL ONE DAY, KEI USED HIS POWERS TO DRAW SLIZZIK, HI-VO, AEGIS, SCRAGG AND MEKARA AND BROUGHT THEM TO LIFE...

...TO BATTLE THE LEVIATHON MOTHER...

...COMBINING THEM INTO SMASHER.

AND IN THE PROCESS?

KEI SAVED THE WORLD.

NOW KEI AND HIS FAMILY LIVE SAFELY ON THE ISLAND OF MU, WHERE KEI'S CREATIONS WOULD BE SAFE AND HE COULD LEARN TO CONTROL HIS POWERS.

ELSA BLOODSTONE, MONSTER HUNTER, NOW GUIDES, PROTECTS AND *TRAINS* KEI.

TOGETHER, THEY PROTECT THE WORLD FROM...

MONSTERS UNLEASHED!

ROBBIE THOMPSON: WRITER
DAVID BALDEÓN: ARTIST
ISRAEL SILVA: COLORS

VC'S TRAVIS LANHAM: LETTERING
KATHLEEN WISNESKI: ASSISTANT EDITOR
DARREN SHAN: EDITOR

MARC SPECTOR.
MERCENARY.
SCOUNDREL. LUNATIC.

HE DIED AT THE FEET OF A STATUE.

MY STATUE.

KHONSHU. THE MOON GOD.

MARC BEGGED FOR HIS LIFE.

I SPARED HIM, AND IN RETURN HE WAS GRANTED MY POWERS. HE BECAME MY CHAMPION ON EARTH.

HE BECAME...

...THE VOICES IN HIS HEAD.

MARC SUFFERS FROM MULTIPLE PERSONALITY DISORDER.

BUT GIVEN TIME, HE HAS MANAGED TO MAKE PEACE WITH THOSE VOICES.

INCLUDING MINE.

NOW, TOGETHER, WE ARE...

MOON KNIGHT

ROBBIE THOMPSON
WRITER

GERMÁN PERALTA
ARTIST

RACHELLE ROSENBERG
COLOR ARTIST

VC'S CORY PETIT
LETTERER

KATHLEEN WISNESKI
ASSISTANT EDITOR

DARREN SHAN
EDITOR

Kamala Khan.

Teenager.

Jersey City resident.

Epic Avengers fanfic writer/consumer.

Awesome at all things higher education.

Not so much at all things fitting in.

This was as close to being a super hero as Kamala ever believed she would come...

...but that was before she realized she carried the *Inhuman* gene.

After she was *exposed* to the Terrigen Mist, her latent *powers* were brought to light and she became...

MS. MARVEL

ROBBIE THOMPSON
WRITER

DIEGO OLORTEGUI
ARTIST

IAN HERRING
COLORIST

VC'S JOE CARAMAGNA
LETTERER

KATHLEEN WISNESKI
ASSISTANT EDITOR

DARREN SHAN
EDITOR

MY NAME IS *LUGAN.*

AND I'M A *MUTANT.*

BEEN A LOTTA THINGS IN MY LIFE.

MERCENARY.

X-MAN.

MURDERER.

I WAS TRICKED INTO *KILLING* MY FELLOW MUTANTS.

BUT I ONLY HAD MYSELF TO BLAME.

AND SO I WALKED AWAY.

PROMISED NEVER TO USE MY CLAWS AGAIN.

AS TIME PASSED, THE WORLD CRUMBLED.

AND IN THE *WASTELANDS,* I FINALLY FOUND WHERE I BELONGED...

...AS A HUSBAND AND A FATHER.

BUT NOTHING GOOD IN THIS WORLD LASTS FOREVER.

I KEPT MY PROMISE. I DIDN'T DRAW MY CLAWS.

EVEN FOR PUNKS LIKE *THE HULK GANG.*

AND IT COST ME EVERYTHING.

I GOT MY REVENGE.

IT DIDN'T BRING MY FAMILY BACK.

NOTHING COULD.

BUT WHEN I WOKE UP IN THE *PAST...*

...IN ANOTHER WORLD, ANOTHER TIME, I REALIZED I HAD A *CHANCE* TO MAKE A DIFFERENCE.

I CAN'T SAVE MY FAMILY, BUT I'LL FIGHT TO SAVE THOSE I CAN.

OLD MAN LOGAN

ROBBIE THOMPSON
WRITER

ANDREA SORRENTINO
ARTIST

LEE LOUGHRIDGE
COLORIST

VC'S CORY PETIT
LETTERER

KATHLEEN WISNESKI
ASSISTANT EDITOR

DARREN SHAN
EDITOR

...BECAUSE FRANK WILL DO *ANYTHING* TO PREVENT ANOTHER FAMILY FROM ENDURING WHAT HE WENT THROUGH. THE INNOCENT WILL BE PROTECTED.

THE GUILTY *PUNISHED.*

FRANK CASTLE DIED WITH HIS FAMILY. NOW, THERE IS ONLY...

THE PUNISHER

ROBBIE THOMPSON
WRITER

MATT HORAK
ARTIST

CHRIS O'HALLORAN
COLOR ARTIST

VC'S CORY PETIT
LETTERER

KATHLEEN WISNESKI
ASSISTANT EDITOR

DARREN SHAN
EDITOR

THE PLANET HALA

BIRTHPLACE OF THE KREE EMPIRE...

...AN ANCIENT AND POWERFUL PEOPLE...

...LOCKED FOREVER IN A WAR WITH THE SKRULL EMPIRE.

THEIR WAR SPREAD THROUGHOUT THE UNIVERSE...

THE KREE EXPERIMENTED ON HUMANS FROM EARTH, DESPERATE TO CREATE A SUPER-SOLDIER THAT WOULD HELP THEM DEFEAT THE SKRULLS.

IN SO DOING, THEY CREATED...

...THE INHUMANS!

THE KREE ABANDONED THEIR CREATIONS. BUT THE INHUMANS THRIVED, CREATING THEIR OWN SOCIETY IN THE CITY OF ATTILAN, LED BY THEIR ROYAL FAMILY FOR CENTURIES.

THEIR OWN EXPERIMENTS WITH THE MYSTERIOUS TERRIGEN MISTS GAVE THE INHUMANS UNBELIEVABLE POWERS.

HUMANKIND EVENTUALLY DISCOVERED THEIR NEIGHBORS. THEY LIVED IN PEACE, AND THE TERRIGEN MISTS CREATED NEW INHUMANS ON EARTH. BUT IN TIME...

...THE INHUMANS DISCOVERED THE TERRIGEN MISTS WERE POISONING EARTH'S MUTANT POPULATION.

THEIR QUEEN, MEDUSA, TOOK IT UPON HERSELF TO DESTROY THE TERRIGEN MISTS ONCE AND FOR ALL.

THERE WOULD BE NO MORE NEW INHUMANS.

MEDUSA ABDICATED HER THRONE.

THE INHUMANS WERE WITHOUT THEIR QUEEN.

BUT THEY WERE NOT WITHOUT SALVATION.

MARVEL BOY, A KREE WARRIOR FROM AN ALTERNATE DIMENSION, CAME TO THE INHUMANS WITH INFORMATION.

INFORMATION ABOUT A SECRET BURIED IN THE REMAINS OF HALA.

A SECRET THAT, IF TRUE, COULD RESTORE THE FUTURE OF THE INHUMANS.

SO MEDUSA, GORGON, CRYSTAL, MAXIMUS (DISGUISED AS BLACK BOLT), SWAIN AND FLINT LEFT EARTH WITH MARVEL BOY TO TRAVEL ACROSS THE STARS. THEY ARE THE INHUMANS' LAST HOPE. THEY ARE...

...THE
ROYALS

HOWEVER, LEGEND OF THEIR JOURNEY TELLS OF SEVEN WHO LEFT FOR THE STARS BUT ONLY SIX RETURNED...

ROBBIE THOMPSON WRITER
KEVIN LIBRANDA ARTIST
DONO SÁNCHEZ-ALMARA
& PROTOBUNKER COLOR ARTISTS
VC'S CLAYTON COWLES LETTERER
KATHLEEN WISNESKI ASST. EDITOR
DARREN SHAN EDITOR

...I WAS IN A COMA FOR WEEKS. WHEN I WOKE, MY WHOLE WORLD HAD CHANGED.

I HAD CHANGED.

AND NOW, WHEN I FEEL RAGE...

...I AM AFRAID.

I AM OUT OF CONTROL.

I AM...

SHE-HULK

ROBBIE THOMPSON
WRITER

DALIBOR TALAJIĆ
ARTIST

MIROSLAV MRVA
COLOR ARTIST

VC'S TRAVIS LANHAM
LETTERER

KATHLEEN WISNESKI
ASSISTANT EDITOR

DARREN SHAN
EDITOR

SPIDER-MAN

ROBBIE THOMPSON
WRITER

VALERIO SCHITI
ARTIST

JESUS ABURTOV
COLORIST

VC'S CORY PETIT
LETTERER

KATHLEEN WISNESKI
ASSISTANT EDITOR

DARREN SHAN
EDITOR

JOHNNY BLAZE.

WITH HIS STEPFATHER DYING OF CANCER, JOHNNY MADE A DEAL WITH MEPHISTO TO SAVE HIS LIFE. IN RETURN...

...HE WAS BONDED WITH THE DEMON ZARATHOS. THE SPIRIT OF VENGEANCE. THE...

GHOST RIDER

BLADE

WHEN ERIK BROOK'S MOTHER WENT INTO LABOR DELIVERING HIM, SHE WAS ATTACKED BY A VAMPIRE.

ERIC WAS BORN PART MAN, PART VAMPIRE. THE DAYWALKER FIGHTS MONSTERS WITHOUT MERCY OR REMORSE.

THE SPIRITS OF VENGEANCE

ROBBIE THOMPSON
WRITER

ANTHONY PIPER
ARTIST

VC'S CORY PETIT
LETTERER

KATHLEEN WISNESKI
ASSISTANT EDITOR

DARREN SHAN
EDITOR

DAILY 🎺 BUGLE
NEW YORK'S FINEST DAILY NEWSPAPER

EVERYONE BLAMED ME FOR PETER'S DEATH...

SPIDER-WOMAN WANTED

...NOBODY MORE THAN ME, THOUGH.

AND SO I'VE DEDICATED MY LIFE TO OWNING UP TO THE *RESPONSIBILITY* GIVEN TO ME WITH THESE POWERS.

I FIGHT FOR PETER, AND FOR ANYONE BEING PICKED ON. FOLKS CALL ME *SPIDER-WOMAN.* BUT YOU CAN CALL ME...

SPIDER-GWEN

ROBBIE THOMPSON WRITER
MARK BAGLEY PENCILER
JOHN DELL INKER
EMILIO LOPEZ COLORIST
VC'S CLAYTON COWLES LETTERER
KATHLEEN WISNESKI ASST. EDITOR
DARREN SHAN EDITOR

HELLO! MY NAME IS DEADPOOL.

A.K.A. WADE WILSON.

A.K.A. THE GREATEST HERO IN THE HISTORY OF MARVEL COMICS.

YOU MAY RECOGNIZE ME FROM MY BEST-SELLING COMIC BOOK, DEADPOOL.

OR PERHAPS FROM RYAN REYNOLDS' INCREDIBLY EXPENSIVE COSPLAY.

NOW, A LOT OF YOU HAVE BEEN WONDERING...

...WHAT IS SPIDER-MAN/DEADPOOL?

WHY, IT'S ONLY THE GREATEST MARVEL COMIC BOOK OF ALL TIME!

IT'S THE CLASSIC TALE OF TWO BROS, TOTAL OPPOSITES, BUT BOTH AS CLEVER AS THEY ARE HANDSOME. THEY'RE DRIVING THE BACK ROADS OF AMERICA, HUNTING MONSTERS AND TRYING TO SAVE THE WORLD.

HEY, IT'S ME. SPIDER-MAN.

DEADPOOL IS MY BEST FRIEND AND ALSO MY IDOL. HE IS ALSO HANDSOME AND WITTY.

WAIT, WHO WROTE THIS GARBAGE--

"NOPE. NOPE. NOPE. NOPE.

DUDE, I JUST GOT MY HAIR DID--

"THIS IS NOT SPIDER-MAN/DEADPOOL..."

ROBBIE THOMPSON WRITER
TODD NAUCK ARTIST
JIM CAMPBELL COLOR ARTIST
VC'S JOE SABINO LETTERER
KATHLEEN WISNESKI ASSISTANT EDITOR
DARREN SHAN EDITOR

DOREEN GREEN!

Doreen was born with the ability to **communicate** with squirrels. How cool is that? What? You don't think it's cool? I mean, it's cooler than being born with the ability to communicate with sloths. Though I'd totally read an Unwakeable Sloth Girl comic. Any-old-who, the squirrels convinced Doreen to use her powers to help people! And you know what? She **did**! You're **welcome**!

Fun Fact: Did you know Squirrels are the smartest animals in the universe? Well, now you do. Because it's a fact. Also a Fact? Nuts are all that matter in life. Nuts. You heard it here first. Tell your friends!

DOOM GOES DOWN!

In Squirrel Girl's first adventure, she totally **saved** her idol Iron Man from Dr. Doom and **proved** she belonged on the big stage! Look out, Avengers, here comes Squirrel Girl!

Fun Fact: Squirrel Girl never did make the Avengers. But she did make the Great Lake Avengers, the 8th or 16th best Avengers squad, where she met me, Tippy-Toe, her partner-in-justice. Also, the real hero of this comic. Seriously, check the wiki--I just updated it while you were reading this.

HOMEWORK IS FUN AND EDUCATIONAL!

Unlike most super heroes (for some reason), Doreen has actually grown **and** grown up...and also gone to college! She's a total genius and not just because she can talk to squirrels, but because she can do math and science stuff. So, when she's not busy saving the world from boredom and alien invasions, Doreen is a student of life **and** computer science!

Fun Fact: I'm still bummed she didn't major in squirrels, but maybe you will? Also, stay in school, kids! Like, seriously, when you're done reading this, do your homework. I'm not kidding. Go. Now.

THUS FALLS GALACTUS!

It usually takes a whole bunch of heroes to take down Galactus, purple fanatic and part-time planet eater--but not Squirrel Girl. She crushed this menace with nothing more than her moxie and her adorable sidekick: me! You're welcome, Earth!

Fun Fact: Did you know Galactus is lactose intolerant? Dude can eat a planet but not a pizza. We all have our crosses to bear.

FRIENDSHIP IS MAGIC!

It's not all punching, kicking and hoarding nuts, though--along the way Squirrel Girl has made friends. And enemies. She's so delightful, she sometimes turns enemies into friends. Because, c'mon, she's awesome. Who doesn't love Squirrel Girl? No really, who? Give me names.

Fun Fact: Despite being a former member of Hydra as well as a raging nihilist, Brain Drain makes a mean veggie burger.

TIPPY-TOE'S GUIDE TO SQUIRREL GIRL CARD 1984 of ∞

UNBEATABLE!

Squirrel Girl is unbeatable. No, like, for realsies. Look at this image! Do your eyes deceive you? Does this text lie to you? No! She beat all these fools by herself. Boom!

Fun Fact: She also beat them with **me.** And lots of squirrels. But yeah, she's totally unbeatable. And totally awesome! So, be like Squirrel Girl! Fight injustice! Be nice to strangers! And stay in school, fam!

Robbie Thompson: Writer   Veronica Fish: Artist   VC's Travis Lanham: Letterer   Kathleen Wisneski: Assistant Editor   Darren Shan: Editor

...THE INFINITY GAUNTLET.

A WEAPON OF GOD-LIKE POWER THAT ALLOWS ITS WEARER TO DO ANYTHING IMAGINABLE.

BUT EVEN AFTER HE LOST IT...HIS THIRST PERSISTED.

ALL OF THE POWER HE SEEKS, ALL OF THE POWER HE WIELDS, ALL OF IT A MEANS TO A SIMPLE AND INEVITABLE END...

...EVERY LIVING THING IN THE UNIVERSE BENDING THEIR KNEES TO THEIR TRUE MASTER...

...THANOS!

ROBBIE THOMPSON WRITER
RON LIM PENCILER
MARC DEERING INKER
ANTONIO FABELA COLORIST
VC'S CLAYTON COWLES LETTERER
KATHLEEN WISNESKI ASST. EDITOR
DARREN SHAN EDITOR

THE HAMMER MJOLNIR BEARS A SIMPLE INSCRIPTION...

"WHOSOEVER HOLDS THIS HAMMER, IF HE BE WORTHY, SHALL POSSESS THE POWER OF THOR."

FOR A TIME, ODINSON WIELDED THE POWER OF MJOLNIR. HE PROTECTED ASGARD AND MIDGARD FROM EVERY FOUL BEAST KNOWN TO GOD AND MAN.

UNTIL HE BECAME...

...UNWORTHY.

MJOLNIR WAITED UNTIL A SUCCESSOR COULD BE FOUND...

JANE FOSTER PURSUED A CAREER IN MEDICINE AFTER LOSING HER MOTHER TO CANCER AT AN EARLY AGE. THE SAME CANCER...

...THAT WOULD ONE DAY FIND JANE.

SHE BATTLED THE CANCER HEAD-ON, NEVER STOPPING.

UNTIL FATE INTERVENED.

CHEMOTH ROO Please Do N

A LONGTIME FRIEND OF ODINSON, JANE ACCEPTED A POSITION IN THE...

...CONGRESS OF WORLDS, A CONGREGATION REPRESENTING THE TEN REALMS. IT WAS THERE THAT MJOLNIR FOUND ITS NEW OWNER.

THOUGH THE TRANSFORMATION CANCELS OUT HER CANCER TREATMENT, JANE HAS ACCEPTED HER NEW LIFE.

FOR NOW SHE KNOWS...

..."WHOSOEVER HOLDS THIS HAMMER, IF SHE BE WORTHY, SHALL POSSESS THE POWER OF..."

THE MIGHTY THOR

ROBBIE THOMPSON WRITER
VALERIO SCHITI ARTIST
RAIN BEREDO COLORS
VC'S JOE SABINO LETTERER
KATHLEEN WISNESKI ASSISTANT EDITOR
DARREN SHAN EDITOR

BUT OUR GENETIC CODES MERGED, GIVING ME ALL OF SPIDER-MAN'S POWERS.

WITH THESE ABILITIES, ALL I NEEDED WAS A HOST...

ROBBIE THOMPSON WRITER
MARK BAGLEY PENCILER
JOHN DELL INKER
RACHELLE ROSENBERG COLORIST
VC'S CLAYTON COWLES LETTERER
KATHLEEN WISNESKI ASST. EDITOR
DARREN SHAN EDITOR

...REVEREND WILLIAM STRYKER BROUGHT THE PROGRAM BACK TO LIFE.

HE HUNTED DOWN MUTANTS LIKE OLD MAN LOGAN, SABRETOOTH, LADY DEATHSTRIKE, DOMINO AND WARPATH...

...AND *STOLE* THEIR DNA IN ORDER TO MAKE...

...EVEN *DEADLIER* WEAPONS.

MUTANT-KILLING MACHINES.

THESE VICTIMS OF THE EXPERIMENTS BANDED TOGETHER TO DESTROY STRYKER'S PROGRAM AND *RECLAIM* THE WEAPON X BANNER FOR *GOOD*.

THEY'VE SWORN TO *PREVENT* THE ABDUCTION, ABUSE OR MURDER OF ANY MUTANT, ANYWHERE IN THE WORLD.

UNITED IN THIS MISSION, THEY ARE...

...WEAPON X!

ROBBIE THOMPSON
WRITER

IBRAIM ROBERSON
ARTIST

ANDY TROY
COLORIST

VC'S JOE CARAMAGNA
LETTERER

KATHLEEN WISNESKI
ASSISTANT EDITOR

DARREN SHAN
EDITOR

...WE WERE *NEVER* GOING TO BECOME WHAT WE BECAME.

WE DECIDED TO *STAY* IN THIS PRESENT.

AND MAKE OUR *OWN* DECISIONS. THE PAST IS THE PAST. AND THE FUTURE BELONGS TO...

...THE X-MEN

ROBBIE THOMPSON
WRITER

MARK BAGLEY
PENCILER

JOHN DELL
INKER

ANDY TROY
COLORIST

VC'S JOE CARAMAGNA
LETTERER

KATHLEEN WISNESKI
ASSISTANT EDITOR

DARREN SHAN
EDITOR

OVER THE YEARS, WE HAVE FORMED MANY TEAMS, FALLEN APART AND REFORMED AGAIN.

I WENT FROM STUDENT...

...TO TEACHER.

AND NOW IT'S FALLEN TO ME...

FOOM! #1

MARVEL

Jeff Youngquist & Brian Overton
editors

Caitlin O'Connell
assistant editor

Joe Hochstein
associate manager, digital assets

Kateri Woody
associate managing editor

Mark D. Beazley
editor, special projects

Jennifer Grünwald
senior editor, special projects

Peter Charpentier
senior manager, merchandising & promotions

David Gabriel
svp print, sales & marketing

Adam Del Re, Rodolfo Muraguchi, Joe Frontirre & Ashley Choy
designers

Jacque Porte, Avia Perez & Elissa Hunter
proofreaders

Axel Alonso
editor in chief

Joe Quesada
chief creative officer

Dan Buckley
president

Alan Fine
executive producer

_____

Thanks to the staff of the original FOOM for the inspiration!

_____

Greetings, O Seeker of Truth, we meet again!

Here in this hallowed circle thou art truly amongst thy peers—thou art truly welcome—thou art truly safe and secure within the fabled, far-flung Fellowship of FOOM*! From this moment on, you are no longer a lonely wanderer on the twisting treadmill of life. Ever at your side stand the rapturous ranks of FOOMdom Assembled! Your days have found new meaning; your nights have been enriched; your world has gained new lustre. Thrice blessed are you, for you have embraced the cause of FOOM forever!

And yet, here in this miniscule moment of eternity, we can but hint at the wonderment that awaits you. Here within the pages you so proudly peruse are contained the words and thoughts, the hopes and aspirations of your fearless fellow FOOMers. Here, clutched within your frantic fingers, are the fruits of a bounty of all that is best, all that is noblest, all that most truly symbolizes the soul and the spirit of we who follow FOOM!

I could parrot the immortal utterances of Smilin' Stan Lee further, but to what avail? Already my limpid eyes grow misty; already the tear-stained page turns soggy in my hand. Only a fellow FOOMer such as yourself can sense the lump in my throat, the deep emotion that threatens to overwhelm me. For, of all the countless words put to paper in days of yore, none have been so fraught with meaning, so tinged with drama, so garnished with glory as these which you now read!

WELCOME BACK TO FOOM
—the best is yet to be!

E Pluribus Marvel!
Tom Brevoort
Master of FOOMonies

stands for "Friends Of Ol' Marvel!"

Greetings, O Seeker of Truth thou hast found thy true Nirvana! Here in the hallowed circle thou art truly amongst thy peers —thou art truly welcome —thou art truly safe and secure within the fabled, far-flung Fellowship of Foom! From this moment on you are no longer a lonely wanderer on the twisting treadmill of life. Ever at your side stand the rapturous ranks of Foomdom Assembled. Your days have found new meaning; your nights have been enriched; your world has gained new lustre. Thrice blessed are you, for you have embraced the cause of Foom forever—now let the angel chorus sing! And yet, here in this miniscule moment of eternity, (O, glorious instant!) we can but hint at the wonderment that awaits you. Here, within the pages you so proudly peruse are contained the words and thoughts, the hopes and aspirations of your fearless fellow Foomers. Here, clutched within your frantic fingers, is the first of many such magnificent magazines which you'll receive—an endless bounty of all that is best, all that is noblest, all that most truly symbolizes the soul and the spirit of we who follow Foom! I could go on and on, but to what avail? Already my limpid eyes grow misty; already the tear-stained page turns soggy in my hand. Only a fellow Foomer like yourself can sense the lump in my throat, the deep emotion that threatens to overwhelm me. For, of all the countless words I have penned in days of yore, none have been so fraught with meaning, so tinged with drama, so garnished with glory as these which now you read—
WELCOME TO FOOM
—the best is yet to be!
Excelsior!
Stan Lee

FIRST ISSUE · SPRING 1973

THE ORIGINAL FOOM

JOE QUESADA, KEVIN NOWLAN & RICHARD ISANOVE

MARVEL LEGACY!

BY JESS HARROLD

Want to know what's so exciting about Marvel Legacy? FOOM spoke to Tom Brevoort and Jason Aaron to find out how their plans will push the Marvel Universe boldly forward, while paying due respect to the storied history of the House of Ideas.

"Marvel Legacy is about touching base with the past as we build toward the future. It's about reminding people about the long history of the Marvel Universe and all of the great characters that have contributed to it over the years. And it's about telling the strongest stories that we can."

That's how Executive Editor Tom Brevoort sums up Marvel Legacy—a line-wide publishing initiative that's been taking shape in secret for months, and over the course of multiple creative retreats. Now, the time has finally arrived for every writer and artist to show readers what they can do.

"We challenged all of our creators to come up with the most exciting storylines that they could, drawing on the history of our characters," Brevoort says. "Stories that would tap into the mythology of the Marvel Universe without just being backwards-looking, which is sometimes the trap. Everybody was encouraged and challenged to bring their A-material to the table and really step things up, to take advantage of this moment to push their storylines forward and do

some remarkable things. So it should be a pretty great period to be a Marvel reader."

Anyone fearing Marvel Legacy is rooted solely in the past can rest assured that isn't the case. "There's nothing wrong with nostalgia," Brevoort says. "But you need to have more than just that in your tank, or it isn't going to carry you very far. So, yes, we're drawing inspiration from some great

ESAD RIBIĆ

storylines and moments of the past—and even hearkening back with things like the old issue numbers and the trade dress and so forth—but we're doing so in the service of telling new stories, stories that will propel the Marvel Universe and its heroes forward. We're embracing the past but focused on tomorrow."

And that's good news for fans of Kamala Khan, Miles Morales, Kate Bishop, Jane Foster, and other heroes who have made their mark in recent years. Brevoort admits he finds it "baffling" to be asked so often whether Legacy will put the focus on "classic" heroes, at the expense of the more diverse cast of modern adventurers. "The Marvel Universe is vast and complex," he says. "There is more than enough room in it for the classic heroes and the newer Marvel icons that we've introduced in recent years. I really don't see how that's even a concern. But that's not to say that absolutely every character is going to be safe—these are Marvel super-hero adventures, and that means there's going to be danger and jeopardy at every turn. And I'd think no differently about the demise of a modern character, if that's where the story took us, than I did of killing the Hulk."

Brevoort is excited to welcome new creators to the House of Ideas, with "great hopes" for Rodney Barnes, who is writing Falcon, and Ed Brisson, who is taking on Cable and Iron Fist. On the art front, both Stefano Caselli (Invincible Iron

Man) and David Marquez (_Defenders_) are doing "next-level stuff," while Juann Cabal on _All-New Wolverine_ "looks to be an exciting new member of our roster."

Sparing a thought for a Marvel stalwart, Brevoort adds: "He tends to get overlooked when you're talking about new creators breaking out, but I feel like Brian Michael] Bendis is really stepping up during Legacy on all of his titles, breathing new energy and excitement into them."

Bendis himself describes Marvel Legacy as "an opportunity for us to tell a story that leaps the characters forward, but the elements of the story are all classic Marvel"—and for more on his books, check out page 12.

As for the characters to watch, Brevoort says _Marvel Legacy #1_ will give readers all the clues they need—but beyond that: It's fair to say that _Mighty Thor #700_ is going to be a big book, even beyond its status as an anniversary issue."

Anyone who's been paying attention will know that those two books have one thing in common. They're both being written by Jason Aaron, one of the finest scribes around. Who better to plot the first chapter of the future of the Marvel Universe than a man who has left his considerable mark on iconic characters including Wolverine, Doctor Strange, and, of course, Thor?

With _Marvel Legacy #1_—and indeed all of his work—Aaron seeks to honor Marvel's rich history and the contributions of the many creators who came before him, in a way that also moves the universe forward, telling stories that haven't been told before. He describes the 50-page one-shot as a "great primer" for everything going on in the Marvel Universe, adding: If you haven't been reading Spider-Man

or Captain America or Thor, or whatever, you can pick up this book and it will give you a tease of where all those characters are at. It kind of sets the stage: This is the Marvel Universe as we know it at this moment in time. And then at the same time, it introduces a couple of new major storylines into the midst of that, things that will begin here and will spread outwards throughout multiple books. This is a book about Marvel's past, present, and future."

As well as showcasing today's greatest heroes, including some who share costumed identities, and setting up a couple of "big dominoes" set to fall in the months to come, Aaron is going deeper into the past than

ever, delving into the "unknown origins" of the Marvel Universe and introducing the prehistoric Avengers of 1,000,000 B.C. This primitive iteration of Earth's Mightiest Heroes is a concept he's been itching to explore for some time, and he's pleased with fan reaction to advance artwork showcasing the roster—particularly a certain flame-haired Spirit of Vengeance astride a woolly mammoth. "_Ghost Rider_ was one of the first things I did at Marvel," he says. "And over the course of that run, I introduced a lot of different versions of Ghost Rider—so this is very much in keeping with that. Ghost Rider's a big part of this _Legacy_ one-shot. And not just this prehistoric Ghost Rider—Robbie

▲ DAVID MARQUEZ & JUSTIN PONSOR

▲ STEFANO CASELLI & MARTE GRACIA

▲ STEFANO CASELLI & MARTE GRACIA

▲ DAVID MARQUEZ & JUSTIN PONSOR

▲ DAVID MARQUEZ & JUSTIN PONSOR

RUSSELL DAUTERMAN & MATTHEW WILSON ▲

▲ STEPHANIE HANS

Reyes also plays a major role here. It's fun to be writing Ghost Rider again, basically!"

No matter the era the story visits, the writer knew he could go "as big and crazy, dark and weird and fantastic as possible" because the book's artist—his *Thor: God of Thunder* collaborator, Esad Ribić—"can nail all of that." He adds: "This one-shot has a really ridiculous, epic scope to it with so many characters, and we zig and zag to so many different parts of the Marvel Universe that there was never any question of what Esad could bring to the table for all that. Plus, there are pages here and there that cut away to different characters, and those are drawn by, for the most part, the artists who are drawing those ongoing series—so it all adds up to being a pretty sweet murderers' row of artists for one book."

But he says it's a "neck and neck race" between *Marvel Legacy #1* and *Thor #700* as to which has the most imposing collection of illustrators. In addition to *Thor* regular Russell Dauterman, the 50-page issue features various versions of the Thunder God, as depicted by talents including Olivier Coipel and the legendary Walter Simonson. It is, as Aaron puts it, an "oversized celebration of all things Thor."

A celebration, but perhaps also a wake. The ominous title above Stephanie Hans' homage variant cover reads: "The Death of the Mighty Thor." But if the end is indeed coming for one of Marvel's most popula new heroes, it shouldn't be a surprise. "Well you know, this is not a new developmen for Jane," Aaron says. "For a while, she' been facing multiple battles—fighting against the forces of evil throughout al the Ten Realms as war spreads, but also fighting a very personal, human battle against cancer. Now we see she's starting to lose one of those battles. That's one o the reasons that she's so worthy to begin with—she knows that being Thor is killing her, but she doesn't slouch. She still goe and picks up that hammer when she need to. That storyline has always been building toward a culmination, and issue #700 i the beginning of that."

To make matters worse for Jane and her allies, Aaron is also unleashing one o Thor's most fearsome enemies—and one of his favorite Jack Kirby creations—i the Mangog. With Malekith continuing to foment the War of Realms, this nex chapter of Aaron's Asgardian epic— which began back in late 2012 with *Thor God of Thunder*—threatens to be the mos explosive yet. "This is maybe the bigges Thor story I've done, the one I've bee waiting to write for years," he says. "I thin it has the chance to be the best one I've ever been part of."

For Aaron, *Marvel Legacy #1* and *Tho #700* are two of the books he is proudes of during his Marvel career—and a platform from which he can swing for ever greate heights. "Together, they set the stage fo what I'll be doing going forward," he promises. "The seeds are planted in *Legac* for my next series, and Thor isn't an ending— it's the next chapter. So if you want to know what I'll be doing come next year for Marvel your answers are in the pages of these two books." True Believers old and new would be wise to pay attention.

MIKE DEODATO JR. ▲

MARVEL LEGACY *Checklist*

ISSUE/NUMBER	STORY/ARC TITLE	WRITER	PENCILER

SEPTEMBER 2017

☐ Marvel Legacy #1		Jason Aaron	Esad Ribić

OCTOBER 2017

☐ All-New Wolverine #25	Orphans of X	Tom Taylor	Juann Cabal
☐ Amazing Spider-Man #789	Fall of Parker	Dan Slott	Stuart Immonen
☐ America #8	Exterminatrix	Gabby Rivera	Joe Quinones
☐ Avengers #672	Worlds Collide Part 1	Mark Waid	Jesús Saiz
☐ Black Panther #165	Klaw Stands Supreme	Ta-Nehisi Coates	Leonard Kirk
☐ Cable #150	The Newer Mutants	Ed Brisson	Jon Malin
☐ Captain Marvel #125	Dark Origin	Margaret Stohl	Michele Bandini
☐ Champions #13	Worlds Collide Part 2	Mark Waid	Humberto Ramos
☐ Defenders #6	Kingpins of New York	Brian Michael Bendis	David Marquez
☐ Despicable Deadpool #287	Deadpool Kills Cable	Gerry Duggan	Scott Koblish
☐ Falcon #1	Take Flight	Rodney Barnes	Joshua Cassara
☐ Iceman #6	Champions Reassembled	Sina Grace	Robert Gill
☐ Incredible Hulk #708	Return to Planet Hulk	Greg Pak	Greg Land
☐ Invincible Iron Man #593	The Search for Tony Stark	Brian Michael Bendis	Stefano Caselli
☐ Iron Fist #72	Sabretooth: Round Two	Ed Brisson	Mike Perkins
☐ Jean Grey #8	Psych War	Dennis Hopeless	Victor Ibáñez
☐ Jessica Jones #13	Return of the Purple Man	Brian Michael Bendis	Michael Gaydos
☐ Luke Cage #166	Caged!	David F. Walker	Nelson Blake II
☐ Mighty Thor #700	The Death of Mighty Thor	Jason Aaron	Russell Dauterman
☐ Monsters Unleashed #7	And Lo There Came...A Poison!	Cullen Bunn	R.B. Silva
☐ Royals #9	Fire from Heaven	Al Ewing	Javier Rodriguez
☐ Spider-Gwen #25	Gwenom	Jason Latour	Robbi Rodriguez
☐ Spirits of Vengeance #1	War at the Gates of Hell	Victor Gischler	David Baldeón
☐ The Unbelievable Gwenpool #21	Doom Sees You	Christopher Hastings	Irene Strychalski
☐ U.S.Avengers #11	Cannonball Run	Al Ewing	Paco Diaz
☐ Uncanny Avengers #28	Stars and Garters	Jim Zub	Sean Izaakse
☐ Venom #155	Lethal Protector	Michael Costa	Mark Bagley
☐ X-Men Blue #13	Mojo Worldwide Part 2	Cullen Bunn	Jorge Molina
☐ X-Men Gold #13	Mojo Worldwide Part 1	Marc Guggenheim	Mike Mayhew

NOVEMBER 2017

☐ Amazing Spider-Man: Renew Your Vows #13	Eight Years Later	Jody Houser	Nick Roche
☐ Ben Reilly: Scarlet Spider #10	The Slingers Return	Peter David	Will Sliney
☐ Captain America #695	Home of the Brave	Mark Waid	Chris Samnee
☐ Daredevil #595	Mayor Fisk	Charles Soule	Stefano Landini
☐ Darkhawk #51	The Return	Chad Bowers, Chris Sims	Kev Wulker
☐ Doctor Strange #381	Loki: Sorcerer Supreme	Donny Cates	Gabriel Hernandez Walta
☐ Generation X #9	OG Gen X	Christina Strain	Amilcar Pinna
☐ Guardians of the Galaxy #146	Infinity Quest	Gerry Duggan	Marcus To
☐ Master of Kung Fu #126	Shang-Chi's Day Off	CM Punk	Dalibor Talajić
☐ Moon Girl and Devil Dinosaur #25	Fantastic Three	Brandon Montclare	Natacha Bustos
☐ Moon Knight #188	Crazy Runs in the Family	Max Bemis	Jacen Burrows
☐ Not Brand Echh #14	Forbush Man Returns!	Nick Spencer, Christopher Hastings, Jay Fosgitt, and more	Jay Fosgitt, Gurihiru, and more
☐ Old Man Logan #31	The Scarlet Samurai	Ed Brisson	Mike Deodato Jr.
☐ Peter Parker: The Spectacular Spider-Man #297	Most Wanted	Chip Zdarsky	Adam Kubert
☐ Power Pack #64	Rarely Pure and Never Simple	Devin Grayson	Marika Cresta
☐ The Punisher #218	Frank Castle: War Machine	Matthew Rosenberg	Guiu Vilanova
☐ Secret Warriors #8	VS Mister Sinister	Matthew Rosenberg	Javier Garrón
☐ She-Hulk #159	Jen Walters Must Die	Mariko Tamaki	Jahnoy Lindsay
☐ Silver Sable and the Wild Pack #36	Silver and Bold	Christa Faust	Matteo Buffagni
☐ Spider-Man #234	Sinister Six Reborn	Brian Michael Bendis	Oscar Bazaldua
☐ Spider-Man/Deadpool #23	Spider-Man Versus Deadpool	Robbie Thompson	Chris Bachalo
☐ Thanos #13	Thanos Wins	Donny Cates	Geoff Shaw

DECEMBER 2017

☐ Black Bolt #8	The Midnight King Returns to Earth	Saladin Ahmed	Christian Ward
☐ Hawkeye #13	Family Reunion	Kelly Thompson	Leonardo Romero
☐ Marvel Two-In-One #1	The Fate of the Four	Chip Zdarsky	Jim Cheung
☐ Ms. Marvel #25	Teenage Wasteland	G. Willow Wilson	Takeshi Miyazawa
☐ Tales of Suspense #100	Red Ledger	Matthew Rosenberg	Travel Foreman
☐ The Unbeatable Squirrel Girl #27	The Forbidden Plo-Nut	Ryan North	Erica Henderson
☐ Weapon X #12	Nuke-Clear War	Greg Pak	Yildiray Cinar

COVER TO COVER

BY JESS HARROLD

▲ ALEX ROSS

▲ ALAN DAVIS, MARK FARMER & MATT YACKEY

▲ JOHN ROMITA JR. & BOB LAYTON

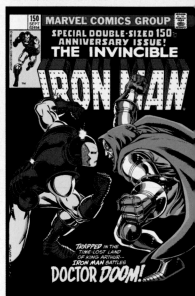

▲ JOHN ROMITA JR. & BOB LAYTON

Legacy celebrates Marvel's glorious past—and limitless future! And what better way to illustrate that than with a series of lenticular homage covers that, with a flick of the wrist, transition between old and new. FOOM takes a good, long look at these modern masterpieces, together with some of the creators involved in bringing them to life!

Fun. That, pure and simple, is what the Marvel Legacy homage covers are all about, according to Executive Editor Tom Brevoort. "To us, it was really just a fun thing to do in the spirit of embracing our roots," he says. "And it's pretty cool to see the whole fleet of them spread out in front of you—like looking at Marvel history all in one go."

Brevoort is delighted to see some classic Marvel character logos back in play on the covers—particularly on *Invincible Iron Man* and *Captain America*—and has enjoyed how the extensive program has given artists the opportunity to "go deeper" into the Marvel catalogue to find covers to homage. "There have been maybe a dozen versions of that *Fantastic Four #1* cover homage over the years, but an homage to, say, *Fantastic Four #2* feels more novel, because it hasn't been done to death—and especially if the source cover bears some relevance to the story being told, you can find some hidden gold there."

And gold there has been, with Brevoort citing Alex Ross' *Captain America #695* cover as his favorite of the bunch—no surprise for a master painter with a flair for what the editor describes as "homages that are more than just homages." What others

would Brevoort want on his wall? "I like the *Jean Grey* cover a lot, the red treatment there is striking, and the *Gwenpool* cover is a fun take on a memorable cover from my youth. I also like Dan Mora's pieces, the *Jessica Jones* cover and the *Champions* cover, both of which similarly go beyond being just a straight-up photocopy of the original."

And Brevoort was happy to share the joy, surprising Brian Michael Bendis with homages to some of the writer's all-time favorite covers on his books. "This is one of the things I love about working at Marvel," Bendis says. "I didn't actually pick any of my Legacy covers. Tom—who has such an encyclopedic knowledge of what

I loved and what influenced me and where my heart lies in the classic stories—used them as my covers. The first being the *Iron Man #150* cover [on *Invincible Iron Man #593*] when Victor and Tony had the time travel story where they went back to King Arthur's court. I love that story and have hearkened back to it a couple of times. And the *Marvel Team-Up Annual #4* Frank Miller cover [on *Jessica Jones #13*]—tha issue is the reason I did *Alias*. That comic meant the world to me as a young man. At the Marvel retreat where they were showing all the covers, mine came up and was like, 'Awww, Tom, I love you.'"

But most inspired of all by the program are

f course, Marvel's talented artists. Perhaps one more so than Michael Allred, whose unique style—a seamless marriage of classic and modern sensibilities—is an ideal fit for Marvel Legacy. "It speaks to me in a very powerful way," Allred says of Legacy. "I'm constantly aware that my earliest memories contain the roots of my deep affection for this storytelling art form and characters who feel like old friends. My goal is to always tap into a timeless classicism while striving to progress and innovate." Seeing the line-wide series of homage covers really "lights up" the fan in him, Allred says. "While I'm always finding new art and creators to get excited about, it's just as exciting to acknowledge the history that everything continues to build on."

For *Avengers* #672, Allred followed in the footsteps of one of the all-time great illustrators of Earth's Mightiest Heroes, John Buscema, paying tribute to his classic *Avengers* #53 cover. Was Buscema one of his big influences as an artist? "Absolutely!" Allred says. "'Big John' Buscema was right up there with Jack Kirby for my older brother Lee and I—especially his work on *Avengers*. He drew some of our most favorite stories with one iconic cover after the other. Of all the great Marvel Bullpen artists, he understood as well as anyone what made Kirby's work pop and solidified the 'Marvel house style.'"

For Allred, the secret to a great homage cover is that it "needs to stand on its own," while also bringing "something new, fun, twisty, or powerful to the party to justify

DAVE JOHNSON ▲

JIM STERANKO ▲

its existence." In his case, the new spin is pitting the Avengers against their youthful counterparts the Champions—but if Allred had any say, the outcome of that battle would be a swift victory for the old order. "That's one contest where the Champions wouldn't be the champs," he says. "Avengers Assemble!"

And assemble they do, alongside the rest of Marvel's greatest heroes across the Marvel Legacy homage covers. Here

are just a few of them—together with the thoughts of some of today's finest talents who took inspiration from the legendary artists that came before them.

Secret Warriors #8 by Dave Johnson, based on *Nick Fury, Agent of S.H.I.E.L.D. #1* by Jim Steranko
Dave Johnson: "Homage covers are kind of fun. Especially when it's a great artist that you're paying tribute to—Kirby,

MIKE MAYHEW ▲

DAVID NAKAYAMA ▲

DAN MORA & MEGAN WILSON ▲

DAN MORA & MEGAN WILSON ▲

MICHAEL ALLRED & LAURA ALLRED ▲

JOHN CASSADAY & LAURA MARTIN ▲

JACK KIRBY & JOE SINNOTT ▲

SAL BUSCEMA ▲

FRANK MILLER & JOSEF RUBINSTEIN ▲

JOHN BUSCEMA & GEORGE TUSKA ▲

▲ MICHAEL RYAN & NOLAN WOODARD

Iceman #6 by Michael Ryan, based on *Champions (1975) #1* by Gil Kane

Michael Ryan: "I had seen the original cover before in a friend's comic collection, but it was bagged and boarded, so I didn't get to read the issue until I found a reprint years later. My goal was really just to switch Hercules and Iceman, but there were unintended consequences that ended with me having to turn Herc's gaze to face out of frame rather than at Bobby—it seems like he might be unhappy having his spot stolen! In homages, the original image being awesome to start with is the main thing, but beyond that I think it's important to understand that you're not trying to copy that image—you're trying to re-create the image with your own set of skills and style."

▲ DAN MORA & ANDRES MOSSA

▲ GIL KANE & DAN ADKINS

▲ STEPHANIE HANS

▲ JOHN ROMITA SR.

Steranko, etc.—and when you get to include the original trade dress. Covers today just don't have that pop-art style that was all about bold action and trade dress and bold fonts. Of course Steranko is an influence. To be honest, I get that comparison a lot—but what most people don't get is that I would say that I was even more influenced by artists from a lot of different time periods, some that Steranko was also influenced by. There were a lot of artists from the sixties that were using trippy iconography. Steranko's genius was to bring current-at-the-time graphic-design ideas into the comics world and make them his own. And the world was better for it."

▲ JIM STARLIN

Mighty Thor #700 by Stephanie Hans, based on *Marvel Graphic Novel #1* by Jim Starlin

Stephanie Hans: "Starlin's cover is a powerful image with an evident reference to Michelangelo's 'Pietà.' I love the almost gothic vibe of this cover compared to the other ones from that period—more symbolic, a bit less straightforward without leaving any doubt about what is in the book. I often use fine art references in comic art. This one is a double-referenced one even, since I had both the original cover and 'Pietà' pictures open at the same time. For a traditional-art nerd like me, it was extremely satisfying."

Ben Reilly: Scarlet Spider #10 by Dan Mora, based on *Amazing Spider-Man (1963) #51* by John Romita Sr.
Monsters Unleashed #7 by Dan Mora, based on *Fantastic Four (1961) #1* by Jack Kirby
Captain Marvel #125 by Dan Mora, based on *Incredible Hulk (1962) #1* by Jack Kirby

Dan Mora: "I'm very excited to be part of it all. The secret of a really good homage is keeping the essence of the original cover but also putting your own stamp on it as an artist. On *Ben Reilly: Scarlet Spider #10*, I love the classic cover composition and the angle on John Romita Sr.'s original, so I just tried to put my mark on it and keep

DAN MORA & ROMULO FAJARDO JR. ▲

JACK KIRBY ▲

JACK KIRBY, GEORGE KLEIN & STAN GOLDBERG ▲

DAN MORA & JESUS ABURTOV ▲

the retro feeling. It was an honor to do the *Monsters Unleashed #7* cover in particular, and the hard part was to maintain the proportions of each hero, given that the new characters are very different in scale. *Captain Marvel #125* was a lot of fun, because Carol Danvers' physique is very different from the Hulk's—that one is my favorite, it is very different from the original but still feels retro."

America #8 by Ben Caldwell, based on *Amazing Spider-Man (1963) #39* by John Romita Sr.
Ben Caldwell: "My favorite super hero was always Spider-Man, so for my 12th

birthday a friend who was a serious collector gave me a mint copy of *Amazing Spider-Man #39*. It was a princely gift, but at the time I didn't fully appreciate it. So a few months later, when a dealer at a convention offered to trade it for a handful of random modern comics, I agreed. The second the deal was done, I regretted it and asked if I could undo it, but no luck. That lost comic has haunted me for the last three decades! Of course I can still read reprints, but it's not quite the same thing. When Wil Moss asked me to do an updated version of that cover for *America*, it was not only a great chance to ape Romita's singular style, but also a bit of self-redemption!"

BEN CALDWELL ▲

JOHN ROMITA SR. ▲

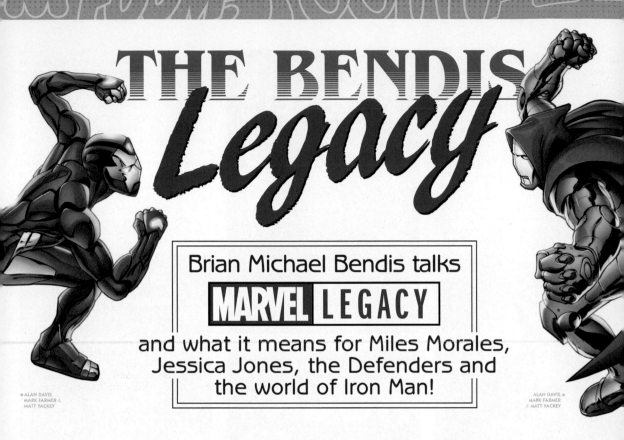

THE BENDIS Legacy

Brian Michael Bendis talks **MARVEL** LEGACY and what it means for Miles Morales, Jessica Jones, the Defenders and the world of Iron Man!

ALAN DAVIS, MARK FARMER & MATT YACKEY

ALAN DAVIS & MARK FARMER & MATT YACKEY

BY **JESS HARROLD**

"Marvel Legacy is an opportunity for us to tell a story that speaks to the vast history of these characters—we get an opportunity to dive in and tell a brand-new story that leaps the characters forward, but the elements of the story are all classic Marvel." That's how an enthusiastic Brian Michael Bendis describes the core philosophy of Marvel Legacy—one that fits him like a glove. In his long career at Marvel, he has always been equally at home delivering revolutionary stories featuring classic characters, such as Daredevil and the Avengers, as he is introducing his own heroes—including Miles Morales, Jessica Jones, and, most recently, Riri Williams. For Bendis, the Marvel Universe is a big place, and Legacy is an opportunity to celebrate both the old and the new. "Just because we're adding new things to the toy box doesn't mean our love for the classic toys is diminished," he says. "In fact, it's the opposite. I see a lot of these newer characters as an extension of our love for Tony or Thor or Hulk—it's a crazy valentine, if anything."

While Marvel Legacy doesn't see Bendis launching a new title, it will majorly influence his four ongoing series (*Invincible Iron Man, Spider-Man, Jessica Jones,* and *Defenders*), but it will do so in tales he was already planning to tell. "I'm really happy about Marvel Legacy because it was where my books were headed," he

says. "For different reasons, because of the story I was telling with Riri and Victor and Tony, 'legacy' is all *Iron Man* was about. Because of Miles and Peter's unique relationship, 'legacy' is what that book is about—Miles' relationship to his parents, his uncle and all that made him who he is. Literally everything I am writing about is about legacy, so it just felt right. When you talk about my long time at Marvel, that

ADI GRANOV

is what it's about. It's amazing how myse and the editorial team have always ha the same goals in mind, whether we discus it or not."

As the new initiative begins, Bend promises that every single one of his book has "a major Legacy moment"—so let take a look at them in turn.

INVINCIBLE IRON MAN

With *Invincible Iron Man* #59. Bendis begins the next stage of his epi exploration of the world of Iron Man— one that has already taken Tony Stark o the board, and seen two characters do their respective armors and take on th mantle. Now, as the saga continues in single title, Riri Williams and Victor Vo Doom are on a collision course. "Loc at *Invincible Iron Man* as an Iron Ma event," Bendis says. "All of the storyline we have been telling about Riri, Victo and obviously the search for Tony Star are slammed together in the very fir issue of our Legacy storyline—so har that there's really no other place to te the story. Everything is converging on thi and it's all going to lead up to a very b page count on #600—it's a runaway tra heading toward that issue. It is the mo unique Iron Man story, it is the bigge Iron Man story, and every single characte involved in it will see a giant change the status quo coming out of it." For far

SANFORD GREENE ▲

"It was that rare occasion where a writer earned his Legacy number all by himself," he says. "I've written every issue that has landed Miles here, so I was happy to own that number because it's a number I'm very proud of." It's an incredible achievement by any standard, even more so when one considers that the title no longer features the same star, and doesn't even take place in the same universe it started in. "We've taken as many bold choices as you can take in the course of the book," Bendis says. "It's amazing that people have stood by it." One reason they have is that Miles Morales is a fascinating character—it's hard not to root for him. "I'm writing a lot of characters that are just figuring out their place in the Marvel Universe," Bendis says. "Riri and Miles particularly are characters that are on a growth-and-discovery arc that is so intense and unique. And that is absolutely what the book is about."

Marvel Legacy follows hot on the heels of another story focusing on, well, legacy: the blockbuster sequel *Spider-Men II* reuniting Miles and his super-hero namesake, Peter Parker. "In that book, Ganke positions Miles to think that maybe some of his troubles are that he's living someone else's legacy," Bendis says. "Like, you're Spider-Man, you kick ass as Spider-Man, even Spider-Man said you can be Spider-Man, but you've been struggling and maybe it's because you're a cover band instead of an original. You're an excellent cover band, you can do 'Stairway to Heaven' as well as Led Zeppelin, but maybe you're not being true to you. And so this idea is out there—and it's a big one, one a lot of people can relate to: artists and writers and anybody who's growing up and doing something because they looked up to someone else who inspired them. You get to a place where you go, 'Now I have to stand on my own two feet.' Is that the story that's happening with Miles? It very well may be. At the same time, Miles and Peter are stars of their *Generations* special, and that's a massive storyline between the two of them. So when we're ready to go on Legacy, huge things will have happened to Miles and Peter that will make Miles' choices going forward just enormous and surprising."

And while Miles is dealing with all that, he'll also have his hands full with a new iteration of a classic Spidey staple: the Sinister Six. "Each one of the Sinister Six has a unique place in Spider-Man history, in the Spider-Man legacy," Bendis says. "And their joining together and their plan is unique to what is going on at Marvel right now. Who the Iron Spider is is a big question, and all will be revealed in the very first issue of the storyline! We've been planning this for literally years, and this Sinister Six story—who these villains are in relation to Miles, what they want from him—is the one that is going to change Miles' life forever, for real, no hype."

Bendis promises that there is more fallout to come from the destruction of the Ultimate Universe that brought Miles to his new home in the Marvel Universe. "One hundred percent," he says. "First of all, he remembers all of it. But how he's handling that, how do you process that? That has a lot to do with this story. A lot of these super-hero kids go through some pretty traumatic things, and they don't deal with them. With Miles it feels more real-world than a lot of super heroes, more intimate—we're in his dorm room, y'know? That gives us the opportunity to delve into what it really feels like to be part of these world-changing events."

JESSICA JONES

No stranger to life-altering super-hero madness herself, Jessica Jones will once again face Zebediah Killgrave—the Purple Man—in Marvel Legacy. "The first Jessica Jones series, which was called *Alias*, all came to a head with the reveal that has been haunting Jessica all her life has been the fact that the Purple Man, this super villain with the power to make you do anything he wants, took over her life," Bendis says. "Not only did he do that, but no one really noticed. It's one of the worst things that's ever happened to a super hero. Now, the only thing scarier than the Purple Man returning is the Purple Man returning when Jessica has healed herself to a place where she can be her version of happily married and have a child. So she has a lot to lose—and the Purple Man doesn't care about any of it. So his return to her life at this time is just about the scariest thing you can think of. On top of that, Jessica as a character is always about the Marvel Legacy—she's looking at the fabric of the Marvel Universe through the gritty reality of the cases that she gets. Jessica in a way embodies everything about Legacy in how she perceives the Marvel Universe."

In *Jessica Jones*, Bendis strives to portray the series star and her husband, Luke

▼DAVID MACK

who have complained about comic-book events not taking place in the main title, he says, this is what they've been waiting for: "I'm looking at Legacy, every single title is the event in the main book. For those fans who've been preaching 'event in the main book,' and I actually agree with them, this is your time to support it with your wallet." Bendis' story will answer the question "Who wields the armor?" as Riri and Victor go head-to-head. The writer adds: "Who's going to be responsible for the legacy if there is no Tony Stark? Who really has to be Iron Man? One person had permission; one person just took it. We'll see where it lands." In the lead-up to the story, Bendis promises that the climactic issue of Victor's book, *Infamous Iron Man #12*, is "gigantic" as the villains behind the scenes and the nature of the former Doctor Doom's goals all come to a head. Stefano Caselli, Alex Maleev and Mike Deodato Jr. will all join him on the path to #600—"everyone who touched the Iron Man book with me will be part of this"—and the anniversary issue will astound fans. "I can tell you that," Bendis says, "because when I told the Marvel creative retreat two of the ideas for Iron Man #600, the room gasped—and that's not an easy room to get a gasp out of."

SPIDER-MAN

While many titles are being renumbered during Marvel Legacy, Miles Morales' book has a unique distinction: Every single one of the issues counted toward *Spider-Man #234* has been written by one man: Bendis. With *Invincible Iron Man*, the scribe played no part in the calculation. But with *Spider-Man*, he wanted it to reflect the full history of the ongoing narrative that began with *Ultimate Spider-Man #1* way back in 2000.

Cage, as a real and believable couple, albeit with super-powers: "One of my goals with Jessica and Luke is to write a complicated, happy adult marriage—about two people who genuinely like each other, and genuinely love each other. It just so happens I'm in a relationship like that—I'm in a very happy marriage—and when I'm reading about marriages or seeing them on TV, I rarely ever see that, that the characters like each other. So I've put it upon myself to make Luke and Jessica teammates in this world, because it's a feeling I can relate to. When we see Luke and Jessica at the beginning of #13, they are actually in a very good place. Getting through the first storylines in this series made them both go: 'No, I want to be married to you. I could have walked away, but I want this.'" Clearly passionate about the book starring one of his signature co-creations, Bendis is also excited that he gets to worth with the same creative team that introduced the character in *Alias*: Michael Gaydos and Matt Hollingsworth on art, with David Mack on covers. As he puts it: "I'll exclude myself from this, but David Mack is a better painter, Mike is a better storyteller and illustrator, and Matt is one of the best colorists of all time. The legacy of the book is that it's the same people making it, but the book is actually better. Fourteen years have gone by since the original—that's an amazing thing that everyone's still alive!"

DEFENDERS

Daredevil and Iron Fist join Jessica and Luke in the pages of Bendis' newest book, *Defenders*—which remains at #6 as Legacy hits, despite being a famous name from Marvel's past. "I could have slapped a big, chunky number on *Defenders*," Bendis says, "but everyone involved went, you know, 'The other *Defenders* book was not this book. It's not the same legacy, so let's just stick to our numbering and focus more on what this Defenders legacy is—which is to defend the streets of the city.'" They may just be starting out doing that together as a team, but things are going to get harder than ever for Luke, Jessica, Matt, and Danny with what Bendis has planned. "The storyline for Legacy is: Who will be the new Kingpin?" he says. "That gives us the chance to just blow the book up. We're going for like a *Godfather* landscape of crime and street-level drama, and we can really open the floodgates in a way that no other book can. The basic fight is Black Cat versus Diamondback. That comes to a big head in #6—from there, what Diamondback has done will wake up a few more candidates who will see that there is serious money to be had. They are going to go for it, so the Defenders, in their attempts to

DAVID MARQUEZ & JUSTIN PONSOR

defeat Diamondback, will cause, not a gang war, but a bloody and scary grab for the Kingpin title. What's really cool, and I think will get people excited, is that not all the good guys stay good guys, and not all the bad guys stay bad guys. There's going to be some serious soul-searching and switching going on, and I think people will be quite startled by who goes where and why, because we're going to see it and their argument is going to be very strong."

The four core Defenders won't be the only ones drawn into the fray, and Bendis teases that the book will have a close connection with *Spider-Man*, where Miles Morales has recently crossed the Black Cat's path. "You're gonna see Miles, Old Man Logan, so many street-level characters," he says. "Blade's already appeared, Elektra. I love this book, it is literally a pile of all my favorite things." And with #6, one of Marvel's highest-profile heroes drops by: a certain Merc whose Mouth seems ideally suited for Bendis to put words into. "It's the first time I have written Deadpool in the sense of 'Let me show everybody how I can write Deadpool,'" he says. "He is a character I have a lot of affection for. I love Gerry Duggan so much that I never even thought to write Deadpool. Now I wanted to do something, and *Defenders* is certainly the place to do it." Bendis pledges to build off the shared history that Duggan has established among Deadpool, Luke, and Iron Fist, but what will Jessica make of Wade Wilson? "Once you become a parent, nonsense—you have no time for it," Bendis says. "Any parent will tell you that. I have four kids, so I have no time for nonsense, but my day is filled with it. So I'm very excited for the scenes between

Jessica and Deadpool, because one i just a big pile of nonsense and the othe is like, 'I've got no time for this.'"

Defenders continues Bendis' creativ partnership with David Marquez, th pair having worked closely togethe since the artist arrived at Marvel. "H came to Marvel with just killer stuf and I jumped on the Marquez train ver early with *Spider-Man*," Bendis say. "David and I have become real friendly he actually moved here to Portlanc and our families became very close Why is *Defenders* such next-level stuff Because we're at the next level of ou creative relationship. This is a book w really want to land and make a uniqu statement with. Not just David and I, bu Justin Ponsor, too. The script is writte as much for Justin as for David—he one of the greatest colorists in comic like a cinematographer."

LEGACY THINKING

For anyone who has followed Bendis career, it's no surprise to hear him spea warmly of his collaborators. He seem to have a knack for building partnership with his artists that are both creativel successful and personally rewarding "In my life, this is where I am inarguabl most spoiled," he says. "Mark Bagley Alex Maleev, David Mack, Sara Pichell David Marquez... I just adore thes people, and my legacy at Marvel wi be these collaborations. Not only am immensely proud of the quality of thes collaborations, I am also immensel proud of those friendships behind th scenes. Comic books are the most fur exciting, scariest collaboration you ca have, and Marvel Comics just allow these collaborations to thrive, from th early days of Stan and Jack to now. It the opportunity to discover things abou ourselves as creators having met thes other creators—things we would neve have found out without meeting them."

So has all the talk of Marvel Legac had him considering the scale of h own contribution to comics? "I try no to involve myself too much," he say: "But the fact of the matter is I do have legacy birthday in 2017, and it's hard no to take stock when you're at a decad marker." Bendis turned 50 in Augus "There we are writing 'Legacy' o everything, and it's hard to connec the dots. There's *Jessica Jones* Seasc Two; there's an animated Spider-Ma movie that Miles is a part of that I' helping with any way I can. So there a lot going on connected to things the I've done at the company that I feel very warm and tingly about. So it nice to be faced with your legacy—and at the same time feel a lot bette about my place in the world than all th characters I write about do!"

TAKE TWO -IN- ONE!

Chip Zdarsky is bringing back glorious comic-book title from the past in **Marvel Two-In-One**! But he's doing it with a twist. Instead of teaming up with a different character each month, now the **Thing** is permanently sharing the limelight with his Fantastic Four buddy, the **Human Torch**. FOOM spoke with Zdarsky about his plans to honor the marvelous legacy of *Two-In-One* and the FF with Ben and Johnny!

▲ JON MALIN & EDGAR DELGADO

By JESS HARROLD

FOOM: *Marvel Two-In-One* recalls fond memories of the 1970s and 1980s, but this isn't anyone's daddy's *Two-In-One*, is it? What's the premise of your book?

ZDARSKY: Yeah, it felt like a good time to bring back the title! Obviously it was originally conceived as a team-up book featuring the Thing and other Marvel characters, but now the *Two-In-One* is more about the Thing and the Torch coming together again to form a unit. After spending time apart following *Secret Wars*, they're the Fantastic Two now, trying to look toward the future.

FOOM: It's been a volatile few years for two of Marvel's true A-list super heroes.

Where are they at right now? What, if anything, is their mission statement?

ZDARSKY: Both of them have tried to move on—with the Guardians, S.H.I.E.L.D., the Inhumans, the Avengers. Part of it is finding usefulness after a life of inherent structure. Part of it is distraction from their belief that Reed, Sue, and the kids have died. It's a huge weight that doesn't go away just from being busy. So I think their mission statement right now is to help each other finally deal with their reality: a world without their family. And where that world can take them.

FOOM: As part of the FF, the two have a small army of iconic villains in their rogues' gallery. Will we be seeing any of them

rear their heads, or perhaps some new rivals for Ben and Johnny to go up against?

ZDARSKY: Yes. Of course! Even though it's not called "Fantastic Four," this is the book that will deal with their villains and allies. And, of course, their main villain turned "ally"—DOOM! Brian Michael Bendis and Alex Maleev have been doing amazing things with him in *Infamous Iron Man*, so it's been a lot of fun writing him here.

FOOM: Even without the rotating guest-star concept, the Thing and the Torch are among the more sociable of Marvel's heroes. Ben's been an Avenger, a Guardian, and the main man of Marvel poker parties. Meanwhile, Johnny's been hanging with the Uncanny Avengers and Inhumans. Surely we'll be seeing a few fellow inhabitants of the MU in this book?

ZDARSKY: Yeah, I mean, I tend to utilize guest stars in my books, and Johnny and Ben make that really easy! This book is about the Marvel Universe and the Marvel MULTIverse, so we'll see some twists on other characters as we go. Both Ben and Johnny are such distinct characters that it's always fun to see them interact with the other heroes. Which is probably why they've ended up on so many teams over the past couple of years!

FOOM: We have to talk about something that fans must be wondering about this book. With Ben and Johnny back together, thoughts inevitably turn to Reed and Sue. What stage have Ben and Johnny reached in the grieving process? Have they accepted they will never see the rest of their family again, or (such is the nature of loss in their world) do they hold out hope? If so, are they on the hunt for answers?

ZDARSKY: Yeah, there's always hope. I mean, they live in a world where both Ben AND Johnny have "died," so that has to mess with your concept of death. But between the two of them, Johnny is the one who most can't let go. He's tried distracting himself, but the weight of what he's lost is catching up to him. He definitely wants answers.

FOOM: As if *MTIO* coming back and you writing it isn't already too much excitement to withstand, you have pretty much the perfect artist on board for this book: Jim Cheung! Is he planning to stick around, and how has it been so far working with a modern-day Marvel legend?

ZDARSKY: Oh, man, I'm hoping we have him for a while! He's one of the best comics artists ever! The detail in his work is breathtaking, but it's never at the expense of story and emotion. The art coming in is blowing me away. I think it's the best work he's done. I think there's a very small handful of people who draw the Thing well, and Jim is on that list.

FOOM: He definitely is! But since you've recently treated fans to some "how to draw" variant covers, how's about you tell us the secret to drawing the Thing and the Human Torch?

ZDARSKY: Look, you think I'm just going to GIVE that kind of info away? Petition Marvel to get me to do one of these covers for *MTIO*!

FOOM: Folks, get writing in! Assuming that, at some point, you have typed or will get to type both of these phrases in a script, which one gives you the biggest tingle of excitement: "It's clobberin' time!" or "Flame on!"?

ZDARSKY: Ha! Catchphrases don't reall give me that tingle. But being able to writ Ben and Johnny as brothers really does. It one of the greatest relationships in comic and I feel pretty lucky to get to write them.

FOOM: Clobberin' aside, Thing has one o the most distinctive "voices" in comics—on that, when written well, makes him one o Marvel's greatest characters, yet one tha comes with the danger of him descendin into parody if it's overdone. How are yo finding it so far?

ZDARSKY: I think, as long as Ben has his ow story, an inner problem that needs solvin that saves you from making him a caricatur of himself. So, basically, you write him c Ben, not the Thing. I hope I manage to na the voice!

FOOM: Johnny has quite the datin history. And for a guy covered in rock Ben is no slouch in that department, eithe Do you have any plans to introduce ne loves for either of our heroes?

ZDARSKY: Oh man, with what happens t them in the first arc? There won't be any tim for romance!

FOOM: No new flame for Johnny c Ben? What a revoltin' development tha is! Can you tease what else is coming i five words?

JIM CHUNG & JUSTIN PONSOR

ALEX ROS

JIM CHEUNG

TWO GOOD TO BE TRUE
Four Fantastic *Marvel Two-In-One* Classics

The original *Marvel Two-In-One* ran for 100 issues between 1974 and 1983 as the Thing stomped his way across the Marvel Universe, making friends with everybody from Man-Thing to…Ben Grimm?! But these four *Two-In-One* team-ups are some of bashful, blue-eyed Benjy's best!

"Death Watch!"
Marvel Two-In-One Annual #2

A key part of Jim Starlin's epic "Thanos War," this action-packed annual paired Marvel's two titans of the team-up, the Thing and Spider-Man, against a literal Titan—and a Mad one, at that! The Thing and Spidey vs. Thanos, drawn by Starlin? If that isn't a collector's item classic, we don't know what is!

"Remembrance of Things Past!"
Marvel Two-In-One #50

Thanks to the magic of Doctor Doom's time machine, Ben heads back to the early days of the Fantastic Four in the hope of finally curing his condition. But his old self isn't too happy to see him, resulting in the clobberin' time to end all clobberin' times. It's rocky Thing vs. original lumpy Thing—as only *FF* legend John Byrne could draw it!

The Project PEGASUS Saga
Marvel Two-In-One #53–58

Who do you ask to work security at a government research center/super villain prison? Why, the Thing, of course! But everything turns to chaos when Deathlok strikes, the deadly Nuklo gets loose, and Thundra leads a group of powerful lady wrestlers in an assault on the facility! Ben will need to call on some of his best MTIO buds, including Quasar, Bill "Giant-Man" Foster, and the wonderful Wundarr! Peril at Project PEGASUS means punches, power players—and poker!

The Serpent Crown Affair
Marvel Two-In-One #64–67 and
Marvel Team-Up Annual #5

Does the power of the Serpent Crown corrupt? Absolutely! So when a fiendish foe gets his hands on two Crowns and threatens to unleash the Serpent-God on Earth, life gets really interesting for the Thing, Stingray, Triton, and Scarlet Witch—culminating in a *Two-In-One Team-Up* with Spider-Man that also draws in Doctor Strange and Quasar! Snakes…why'd it have to be snakes?

ZDARSKY: Secrets. Adventure. Doom. Betrayal. Mole.

FOOM: So let's cut to the chase, then. *Marvel Two-In-One* is the new World's Greatest Comics Magazine, right?

ZDARSKY: Look, far be it from me to weigh in on matters that are, ultimately, to be decided on by the World Comics Magazine Supreme Court, but I think we have a strong case here.

Give your verdict when *Marvel Two-In-One* returns this December!

MARK BROOKS

AVENGERS WRITERS ASSEMBLE!

BY **JESS HARROLD**

Mark Waid, Jim Zub, and Al Ewing share their plans to take *Avengers*, *Uncanny Avengers*, and *U.S. Avengers* into Marvel Legacy, before combining all three titles into one weekly book starting with the landmark *Avengers* #675—and the epic "No Surrender"!

FOOM: Beginning with Mark, Marvel Legacy sees a crossover between your Avengers and Champions teams. It looks like they're going up against the High Evolutionary, but will the two teams be fighting for the same thing? Or in classic comic-book fashion, will there be some disagreement?

MARK WAID: The team-up encapsulates everything legacy means to Marvel. The classic generation and the younger generation have to put their differences aside, yes—but more than that, the Champions have to work hard not to be unconsciously marginalized by the Avengers. The center of all the friction is the Vision/Viv relationship, which as

we see from the very first pages is in a rocky, ugly place. Whatever's happening between them seems to transcend a normal "father/teenage daughter" clash, and that tension spills out over both teams.

FOOM: Jim, with *Uncanny Avengers*, you're putting the focus on a classic Marvel bromance that unites the worlds of Avengers and X-Men: Wonder Man and the Beast. A lot has changed for both of them since their Avengers glory days—how's their friendship doing?

JIM ZUB: Hank and Simon have been through a lot since they had any time to hang out and commiserate. The fact that Simon has been away (lost as ionic energy absorbed by Rogue) for quite a while allows him a different perspective compared to Hank, who has been in the trenches for some of the biggest recent events of the Marvel Universe (the return of the original X-Men from the past, the M-Pox and battle with the Inhumans for mutant survival in *IvX*, and war between the Hydra Nation and New Tian in *Secret Empire*). In short, Beast has made some big

mistakes and is trying to figure himself ou[t] Simon thought he had his life sorted but the[n] was pulled away, and the world moved o[n] without him. They're both looking for clarit[y] and redemption in their own ways. Seeing ol[d] friends and taking stock of where your life [is] at and what you need to do next echoes th[e] other stories happening with the Uncann[y] Avengers and Marvel Legacy as a whole.

FOOM: And what's going on with th[e] rest of the Uncanny team?

ZUB: The Unity Squad were officiall[y] disbanded by Steve Rogers in the build-u[p] to *Secret Empire*, but they kept operating o[n] their own with shared purpose and a sens[e] of loyalty to each other. No charter, n[o] membership IDs, no home base. Now the[y] need to decide if they formalize that tea[m] structure once again or go their separat[e] ways. Rogue, Wasp, Synapse, Docto[r] Voodoo, Quicksilver, and the Scarle[t] Witch will all be in the mix here, rebuildin[g] after *Secret Empire* and planning for th[e] future while dealing with the unexpecte[d] arrival of villains from their past. Ther[e]

GEE, MISTER! WHAT'S *YOUR* STORY?

WHATEVER IT IS, TELL **ME** FIRST!

DAVID NAKAYAMA ▲

will be plenty of love and loss, conflict and calamity in the months to come.

FOOM: Al, where do recent developments leave the U.S.Avengers?

AL EWING: They are heading out of *Secret Empire* and the aftermath issue in a state of flux—between Hydra machinations and more banal evils, the team has been put through the wringer, and one or two of them won't ever be the same again. Also, readers can expect a new Supreme Leader of A.I.M.—but what does that mean for Roberto Da Costa? You'll find out.

FOOM: Your first Legacy cover promises the search for Cannonball. And it looks like that's going to include a trip to a planet that evokes a certain other comic book world beloved of Mark Waid...

EWING: We are veering toward a certain "Typical Teenager," yes—it's one of those things that just fell together as the story coalesced out of the ether. It's not meant as a parody, exactly—I dig what the Archie books are doing right now—but I am finding that riffing on that classical Americana, and pairing it with sinister and alien undertones barely beneath the surface, can make for some enjoyably creepy moments. I've only written a little bit of "Ritchie Redwood," but he's turned out to be an oddly magnetic and terrifying presence so far.

WAID: WHAT? I need to catch up on my reading.

FOOM: And when Mark does that, Al, what will he encounter with the rest of the U.S.A. squad?

EWING: There are a few changes to our

merry gang of misfits. One member's powers aren't fully under control, one member's powers are much more under control, and one member has given up their super-hero identity entirely. Also, fans of solicits will have noticed the Shi'ar Superguardian Smasher (her name is Smasher; she doesn't smash Superguardians) is joining the team during the search for Cannonball. Something for readers who like mom-and-pop super-hero pairings there, as well as big spaceships.

FOOM: So how many issues do you all have before we get to the big one—*Avengers* #675—and Earth's Mightiest Heroes go weekly?

WAID: *Avengers* #674 is a finale for the current team as it exists—Falcon, Spider-Man, Hercules, Wasp, Thor, and Vision—because, as is a staple of *Avengers* storytelling since #16, the old order is about to changeth...

ZUB: *Uncanny Avengers* #30 is our final issue before the weekly format of "No Surrender" launches. We cover a lot of ground between now and then, tying up old threads, rebuilding old bonds, and setting the stage for our epic adventure in *Avengers* #675 and beyond.

EWING: Issue #12 is going to be the last issue of *U.S.Avengers*, then we're taking a month break, and after that the team has a very big role to play in "No Surrender"—but will it be their last? Who will survive, and what will be left of them? Kill your darlings, they say...

FOOM: Uh-oh! How are you all approaching the collaboration on the new "No Surrender" era?

TERRY DODSON & RACHEL DODSON ▲

ZUB: Mark, Al, and I have been planning this massive weekly storyline since the start of the year. We met up with Tom Brevoort and Alanna Smith in New York for an Avengers summit in February, and things quickly went from concept to execution. It really is an "all hands on deck" collaborative effort between the writers, artists, and editorial team with spreadsheets showing where characters are at and where they're going throughout the story, diagrams and new character designs, location floor plans, references from dozens of past Avengers stories—you name it. It's been a wild ride but also a ton of fun contributing to such an important new chapter in Avengers history.

EWING: We're all working together—some issues, one of us has more pages, some issues that same person will have less—but it's all essentially an equal share, and we're all bringing our own particular skill sets into the mix. I'm finding it fairly reminiscent of previous collaborations—"Trifecta," the Judge Dredd crossover story in 2000 AD in particular, as that was another weekly, three-person job with a lot of connecting parts.

WAID: I was brought aboard as a key player in the very first successful American weekly comic, albeit from another company, so I'm very comfortable with co-plotting and divvying up sub-assignments within the overall work. We do all tend to "land" on certain characters, shepherding certain ones—Al tends to handle the Red Wolf beats, for example, and I lean toward the Jarvis beats—but everyone gets a say in everything, and everyone's voice is heard. Even Brevoort's.

FOOM: What can you tell us about "No Surrender"?

ZUB: "No Surrender" marks the final hurrah for this era of Earth's Mightiest Heroes. Beyond that, you'll just have to wait and see.

WAID: It's half celebration, half wake.

EWING: Some endings are also beginnings. Mind you, some are just endings...

FOOM: Sounds ominous. Will the three squads continue to operate separately, or are we seeing a transition back to the days of one true Avengers team?

ZUB: I don't think it's too much of a spoiler to say that the teams start the story independent and quickly realize their combined efforts will be needed to tackle the Earth-shaking threat at the core of our story.

FOOM: The classic statue of the founders is central to the teaser image—is it fair to say that this story resonates with the history (indeed, the legacy) of the Avengers?

ZUB: Absolutely. "No Surrender" is being built as a milestone that reflects on the past even as it looks toward the future. Old Avengers fans and new will find a lot to love here.

WAID: You can't tell a story of this scope and with this impact without considering all the eras of the Avengers past and present. Certain clues as to what's going on can be found in the past as well as in the present day, so it's critical that we give context.

EWING: And in terms of the legacy, we're adding some big, beautiful new pieces to the Marvel Universe with this series. I could definitely see a couple of these new creations being part of Avengers stories in the future—although that might depend if the Avengers have one.

FOOM: What can you tell us about some of the key Avengers in the story, and why they're major players?

ZUB: Quicksilver is in a dark place at the start of "No Surrender." He's looking for a way to prove himself in the days ahead.

WAID: Also, I have an affinity for writing super-speed characters. Go figure.

ZUB: Rogue thinks she's focused and ready for the challenges to come, but this battle is going to take something special from her. Beast is trying to reconnect to a time in his life when he knew who he was and what he stood for. The Avengers are a big part of that journey.

WAID: In a giant Avengers team this powerful, Beast quickly realizes that he serves best as a scientist, not a super hero—and the discoveries he makes alongside the Wasp will be crucial to the team's survival.

EWING: Vision gets some interesting beats over the course of the story. He's deeply connected to the history of the Avengers—not to mention that as the android Avenger, he can be a living communications hub between the three very different active teams. Which might put him in the firing line for some dark forces...

FOOM: Is that Living Lightning we can see, too?

EWING: That is Living Lightning—or just "Lightning," these days. He's someone who was an Avenger, but drifted away from the team, and is now re-examining that decision. I felt like it was a good idea to have someone coming back to prove the whole "once an Avenger, always an Avenger" thing—plus he's got some pretty cool powers, so it's a crime he's not used more often. He's joining us in #675 with his own supporting cast and even a little bit of romance. He hasn't just

been sitting in a green room waiting to get the call all this time, he's been off having exciting adventures—and filling out suits really well.

FOOM: Are any other characters primed to make a big splash in "No Surrender"?

WAID: Jarvis. If you look at all of Avengers history as one long story, Jarvis is the through-line. He's been involved in every incarnation of the team, observing from the sidelines, and his knowledge of Avengers history will, at a key point, be critical to Earth's very survival.

EWING: Everyone gets their moment in the sun in this book—any reader coming into this from one of the current Avengers books will get to see their favorite characters from those books doing some cool things at some point in the story. For instance, Mark mentioned some Red Wolf beats earlier—in one of the issues, he gets a particular moment to shine that I'm hoping fans of his will enjoy. And we have a whole crew of bad guys, too—some old faves and some new faces I think you'll love.

ZUB: We have some new characters, both heroic and villainous, that we're really excited to unveil. Beyond that, the crew you see in the Alex Ross piece is central to the story, as well as at least two Avengers founders—but not necessarily the ones you'd expect.

FOOM: Who are the artists assembled to bring this story to life?

ZUB: Pepe Larraz is drawing month one of the story, bringing the same incredible storytelling and dynamic action fans have grown to love in *Uncanny Avengers*. Some of the scenes we've given him to draw to get this story underway have been staggeringly difficult, and he's delivered on them with style and grace beyond our wildest expectations. Seriously, this is career-making work for Pepe. Readers are going to freak out.

WAID: Kim Jacinto is drawing month two. He's my personal hero for bringing both the humanity and the bombast to a cast of roughly one billion characters. His eye is amazing when it comes to picking just the right split seconds to illustrate, and the way he handles action is remarkable. Couldn't be happier to have him aboard.

EWING: Paco Medina joins us for month three, making it a particularly favorite month for me personally. Fans of his immaculate art style will very much dig the big action beats of his issues—but there are also some chilling moments verging on horror mixed in, which is a little new for us, so I'm looking forward to what he does

with that. *U.S. Avengers* fans will be deeply satisfied, I think—as will everyone else.

FOOM: It all sounds great, but imagine you're talking to one person who loves the movies but has never read an Avengers comic, and another who once loved the title but hasn't read an issue in years. Why should they buy this book?

WAID: To the movie-lover, as big as the Avengers stories have been on the screen this one's even more epic. We're all seasoned storytellers, so we promise you that you'll never be lost or confused—just thrilled. And to the returning fans, if there's a former Avenger you ever loved, s/he's going to have an active role, whoever it is.

EWING: This is a big-budget Avengers spectacular, filled to bursting with new and cool characters as well as a whole bunch of your cinematic favorites—and if we're doing our jobs, you'll be able to pick it up from page one and dive right in. To Avengers fans of old, there have been some developments since you were last with us, but the basics haven't changed. There has come a day—a day unlike any other—and Earth's Mightiest Heroes will answer the call, assemble and do what they do best in the face of overwhelming odds. Join us for the faces you know—we'll make you fall in love with the ones you don't. That's a *promise*.

ZUB: Al and Mark have said it all right there. At this point in the collaborative process we've become a hive mind, so they knew what I would say before it ever reached my mouth. By the time you read this, Mark and Al have written my weekly to-do list and reminded me about my upcoming dental appointments. Go Team Avengers.

ALEX ROSS

KELLY THOMPSON HITS THE BULLSEYE WITH HAWKEYE

LEONARDO ROMERO & JORDIE BELLAIRE

BY JOHN RHETT THOMAS

As the Kate Bishop—starring *Hawkeye* aims for its Legacy launch, *FOOM* decided it was perfect timing to check in with the series' writer, Kelly Thompson. Want my opinion? *Hawkeye* is one of Marvel's best series, and Thompson is one of its rising stars. Building on the success of Matt Fraction and David Aja's Eisner Award—winning series that matched Hawkeye (Clint Barton) with Hawkeye (the aforementioned Kate), Thompson and her creative partners maintained a similar vibe in what I find to be, as the writer puts it in our interview, an "eminently readable and lovable series." We talk about all that and more, including her comic-nerd bonafides (hint: she's a bigger fan of Rogue and Gambit than you are!), her background as a writer, and, of course, Hawkeye.

FOOM: What were some of your favorite comics/characters when you started reading as a teenager?

KELLY: I was hardcore for the X-Men as a teenager. And Rogue and Gambit were especially close to my teen heart. I had not only a copy of *X-Men #24* framed in my room, but I had bought extra copies of both *X-Men #24* and *Gambit #1* and cut them up and made a framed collage as well. Can you say...SUPERFAN?!

FOOM: What about those characters clicked with you?

KELLY: I think—broadly—the X-Men connected with me then for the same reasons they click with people now: They're outcasts and misfits (something we all feel, but we feel especially as teens, I

ANDY KUBERT & MATTHEW RYAN

suspect), and they built their own amazing powerful family together. Specifically fo Rogue and Gambit? I NEEDED THEM TC KISS. I NEEDED IT SO BAD!

FOOM: Your blog bio says you went to Savannah College of Art & Design to ge a degree in sequential art. Were you intent on being an artist? Do you have any art skills under your belt that you've used in comics at all? Or wish to use?

KELLY: When I first discovered comic as a teen, I was elated because I had always wanted to be a writer, and comic was such a fascinating merging of word and pictures that I became really excited about the idea of that specific art form. I made me think perhaps I could do it. Bu I'm not a terribly talented artist, and while with practice I'm sure I could have gotter better, I doubt I ever could have reached the heights I aspired to. However, wit lots of writing practice, I do have hope that I can achieve those equivalent writing heights. And yes, everything I learned about art (and in trying to be an artist helps make me a better writer—especially as it comes to breaking and pacing a story

FOOM: It has been five years since you self-published your debut novel *The Girl Who Would Be King*. Looking back what do you make of the success of tha novel, and how much longer 'til you think you'll have a sequel complete?

KELLY: Oof! You're not pulling any punches! I think *TGWWBK* first and foremost taught me a lot about both writing and about publishing. The success of that book also opened some doors for me and helped me financially make some progress in becoming a full-time writer. I put off the sequel for a long time as the book was in different stages of being optioned to be a movie or a TV show (as these things sometimes do), and in the meantime I moved on to another series (*Storykiller*), but I have recently decided to return to the sequel (*The God Slayer*). I hope it will be out in 2018 with *Storykiller 2*, early 2019 at the latest. Fingers crossed!

FOOM: How did working at Marvel fit into your plans as a writer? Was this even something you'd dreamed of doing?

KELLY: Absolutely. I think from the first time I saw Rogue in the '90s animated series punching that Sentinel in a mall I knew I was connecting to something powerful within me. And when I found comics (thanks to my younger brother, Scott) a few weeks later, I knew I wanted comics to be my life. Marvel comics were my first loves. I even wrote a letter to Marvel when I was a teen. Comics is a very fast-paced industry, so I have struggled in these first years with finding time for novels in between comic-book deadlines, but I'm optimistic that I'm getting better at it.

FOOM: Of the Marvel Legacy books you've heard news of, which are you most excited about?

KELLY: I mean, *Hawkeye*, obviously! Just kidding. I've been loving Tom Taylor's *All-New Wolverine*, so I'm really excited for what's going to happen over there. I also am always here for *Jessica Jones*. *Ms. Marvel* is always powerful, and the new *Guardians* book has been excellent so I'm interested in checking that out, too.

FOOM: *Hawkeye* has been in excellent hands since Matt Fraction and David Aja took it to crazy heights of critical acclaim. Your series seems to be a continuation of that storytelling excellence.

KELLY: What we're doing is definitely a direct spiritual descendent from the Fraction/Aja/Wu/Hollingsworth stuff—especially the Kate in L.A. stuff. Their *Hawkeye* book is one of my favorite comic books of all time. I think it brilliantly reinvents itself (and super-hero books). It's smart and funny and emotional all at once, and it plays with (and breaks in half) narrative and structure and visuals and expectations in a way that seems effortless (though I'm sure it was not). Stepping into

▲ DAVID AJA & MATT HOLLINGSWORTH

that shadow is scary—it's a very deep shadow. But you just try not to think about it too much. You try your best to honor what came before while doing your own thing as much as you can. I am very lucky to have an incredible team to help me do that, creatively and editorially. I feel like we all came together with a really beautiful cohesive vision, and I couldn't be prouder of what we've done, despite very big shoes to fill.

FOOM: Leonardo Romero seems a perfect fit as the artist for your stories. It's plainly a super-hero book, but he also manages to convey the humor (sometimes subtle, sometimes slapstick)

▲ LEONARDO ROMERO & JORDIE BELLAIRE

of your stories.

KELLY: I am insanely lucky to have my team. Leo is a magnificent artist—a true talent—and he's a very good match for both *Hawkeye* and for me as a writer. He is the rare comic-book artist that can handle big super-hero stuff with the same ease as more street-level stuff, and since Kate's book is both, she needed that kind of artist. And I knew that from the beginning—that he was that kind of artist—but what I didn't know when we first began was how much Leo would "get me" and the sense of humor and fun I was trying to bring to Kate. But he gets it SO MUCH. And he makes everything I try to do about a hundred times better than it has any right to be.

FOOM: And let's not forget colorist Jordie Bellaire. What's your sense of what she brings to the table artistically?

KELLY: Ah, Jordie. My kingdom for a million Jordie Bellaires. She's a dream. When we were all first talking about the look of the book, and I was describing the tone and ideas behind the book, she goes (paraphrasing here), "So Hollywood neo-noir meets *Miami Vice*," and we all went "YESSSSSS." She never disappoints, and much like Leo, just when you think she's done the best work she can do, she one-ups herself.

FOOM: Those covers by Julian Totino Tedesco are amazing. A really great sense of design style. Do you have a favorite (or three)?

KELLY: Oh man, Julian! Like everyone on our team, he's just totally bringing his A game to every cover. He has so nailed that perfect pulp-detective look for our book, and I adore it. If I had to pick a few favorites—probably *Hawkeye #1*, *Hawkeye #2*, *Hawkeye #7* (also my favorite issue, period), and the upcoming *Hawkeye #10*.

FOOM: How would you sum up Kate Bishop, her personality and her hero skills, to someone that's never read *Hawkeye*?

KELLY: Kate Bishop is all sass and never-give-up moxie. She's an extremely gifted bowman, and has a boatload of other talents, too—but she's also extremely flawed and relatable. She's a hero through and through, and she doesn't give up until she wins. Thus, she always wins. (*Laughter*.)

FOOM: Kate has a "go get 'em" attitude that routinely places her into sticky situations—but she also has a resolve and resourcefulness that serves her well in getting out of them. She's up for the challenge, in other words, even if she's

Kelly Thompson · Leonardo Romero

hawkeye

The adorable archer takes aim— ON DANGER!

399¢

JULIAN TOTINO TEDESCO ▲

still learning, and that's endearing about her character.

KELLY: I like to think this "go get 'em" aspect of Kate is something that she and Clint share so deeply that it's basically become a quintessential Hawkeye trait. It's part of how they can survive considering they're often the (technically!) least powerful people in any super-hero scenario. They hold their own against the biggest bads in the universe, and alongside some of the most jaw-droppingly powerful heroes—and they do it with a shrug and the confidence of twenty heroes.

FOOM: The comic is set in Venice Beach, Los Angeles. Have you spent much time there? Any comments on what the setting/locale brings to the stories you tell?

KELLY: Yeah, I'm from California originally, and I lived in L.A. after college for about five years before moving to Manhattan. I love it there. I haven't been back in a while, so my version of L.A./Venice is likely a bit dated, but I think I still have a good grasp on what makes it such a special place, and I try my best to bring that unique California energy to the scripts. However, Leo and Jordie are the ones that really capture it so perfectly.

FOOM: The two-part Jessica Jones run shows a real kinship between the two characters. Definitely some hero worship there. How much of Jessica Jones' past did you model Kate's P.I. pursuits after?

KELLY: Well, I think Kate and Jessica are very different people, and thus they're very different P.I.s, but Kate absolutely looks up to Jess and knows that not only does she (Kate) have a lot to learn, but Jess has a lot to teach. They were magic together. I loved every minute of it, a real perfect chemistry in how they played off one another.

FOOM: One of the themes of your *Hawkeye* run is what are called "anchor points." In Kate's usage, it means the people who keep her grounded and focused on taking on life as it comes. When the book takes on its Legacy branding, what are the anchor points going to be? The dynamics of the supporting cast have been pleasingly slow simmering.

KELLY: Clint is and always will be one of Kate's primary anchor points, which is to both good and ill effect. Clint is a good man, mentor, and hero, but he's also a bit of an irresponsible and unpredictable wild card, and it's hard for that to be a point of stability for someone. Some of Kate's other anchor points (that have been breaking) are her family, and we'll be dealing with that in a big way for Legacy. It's hard to share a book with Kate—she shines so bright!—but she's built up a good little base of friends as her "L.A. family," and they have absolutely become new anchor points for her—she'll go to extreme lengths to protect them.

FOOM: Can you tease some of the guest-stars or bad guys we'll see as Kate's Legacy adventures unfold? Will Hawkguy

make the scene? Any of her Young Avengers pals? More Jessica Jones?

KELLY: I think at this point I'm allowed to say that for *Hawkeye #12*, which is a standalone issue before we launch into our Legacy storyline, we'll be having Wolverine (Laura Kinney) and Gabby (! teaming up with Kate in L.A. for a quick mission. It was really fun to write, and we have our Jessica Jones guest-arc artist Michael Walsh coming back, so that was really exciting for us. After that, for our Legacy arc, we've got Clint coming back onto the book—and I'm so excited about that. They have such a magic chemistry together. I'd love to have America and/or some of her Young Avengers crew pop up, but we'll have to see what happens after the Legacy arc.

FOOM: Returning to the sense of humor in your writing style, it seems to have the perfect amount for a super-hero book that doesn't take itself too seriously but is still serious about the super-hero stuff—if that makes sense! What kind of sense of humor do you think Kate relies on? She's at times goofy/sardonic/sarcastic/whimsical...

KELLY: One of my favorite things we've been doing in this latest arc is that Kate is "off"—because she's going through some big emotional things, she's not quite her usual self, and her friends/colleagues have noticed. And yet, even with her being off, she never stops being the indefatigable Kate. She has an almost absurdly boundless optimism and "can do" attitude, and even at her worst, it gets her through. In fact, I think it's when she's at her worst that her attitude and approach to life actually propels her, helps her survive. Jessica Jones said in *Hawkeye #6* that Kate likes to "make her own fun," and it's really true. And that aspect makes her eminently readable and lovable.

Kelly Thompson · Leonardo Romero · Jordie Bellaire

hawkeye

WHERE TROUBLE LURKS, BISHOP WORKS!

JULIAN TOTINO TEDESCO ▲

Kelly Thompson · Leonardo Romero · Jordie Bellaire

hawkeye

Who's the DEADLIEST of them all?

JULIAN TOTINO TEDESCO ▲

Kelly Thompson · Leonardo Romero · Jordie Bellaire

hawkeye

The Enemy

JULIAN TOTINO TEDESCO ▲

DEADPOOL'S GUIDE TO DEADPOOL!

Want to read Deadpool comics but don't know where to begin? Well, who better to ask but the man himself! And the good thing is, he's his own favorite subject. Exclusively for FOOM, Wade Wilson selects some choice tomes from his personal library—no, not that personal library, we're talking his collected-editions stash! (As told to Jess Harrold.)

For some reason, these last couple of years, more and more people are stopping me on the street to say: "Deadpool, we love you! Where can we find more of your zany adventures?" They also shout "maximum effort" at me like it's some sort of catchphrase. People are weird. But anyway, when FOOM called asking me to pick my own favorite Deadpool collected editions, I figured, hey, that's a great way to answer all my adoring fans in one go—so maybe I can get some peace. Maximum reward, minimum effort. Now there's a catchphrase. Without further a-doo-doo, on with the books!

1 DEADPOOL: BEGINNINGS OMNIBUS HC
New Mutants (1983) #98, Deadpool: The Circle Chase #1-4, Deadpool (1994) #1-4, and more!

Let's start at the very beginning, which a singing nun once told me is a very good place to start. This book kicks off with the collector's classic *New Mutants #98*, in which Rob Liefeld and Fabian Nicieza somehow took my life and put it on the printed page, changing the course of comics history—forever! Rob did an awesome job of capturing my glorious image, though I could have used more pouches. The ladies dig pouches. Across this volume, see how I went from standing on Cable's (not inconsiderable) shoulders, to stealing the show in his red-hot *X-Force* and other books, to taking my own fledgling steps into solo superstardom in my first two limited series.

2 DEADPOOL BY JOE KELLY OMNIBUS HC
Deadpool (1997) #1-33 and more!

This is where I really found my voice—and the extra-strength yellow word balloons it takes to contain it. Comic-book historians (they're the ones who flunked out of history in college) speak of certain creators' runs in reverently hushed tones. Miller on Daredevil. Simonson on Thor. Ditko on Speedball. When it comes to Kelly on Deadpool, they speak in giddy excitement, stifling guffaws.

Ed McGuinness on art sure could capture my good side, while Joe had a way of bringing it out, setting me on my heroic path to glory.

3 DEADPOOL & CABLE OMNIBUS HC
Cable & Deadpool #1-50 and more!

Back when this series first came out, would you believe top billing went to ol' Nathan Christopher Charles Dayspring Askani'son Stormborn of the House Summers, First of His Name, the Unburnt, Breaker of Chains, Mother of Dragons... Wait, I might have gotten distracted there. Let's just call him Cable. Well, it's Deadpool first on the Omnibus, one-eye! As for the contents, who better than Fabian Nicieza to reunite two great tastes that explode things great together—and recapture the volatile chemistry that made me and Cable icons of the nineties. If they remade *The Odd Couple* with, say, Ryan Reynolds and Josh Brolin, and

threw in lots of guns, time travel and Bea Arthur jokes, they'd end up with something a little like this.

4 DEADPOOL BY DANIEL WAY OMNIBUS VOL. 1 HC
Wolverine: Origins #21-25, Deadpool (2008) #1-26, and more, on sale in February 2018!

When it comes to writing my adventures, there's no right way, and there's no wrong way. But there is a Daniel Way—and that involves not one, but two voices in my head. With my thoughts more confused than ever, and whacked-out hallucinations making matters even worse, Way picked a great time to slam me up against Wolverine in a knock-down, drag-out battle of guns, claws, swords, bazookas, bombs, and...a piano. Seriously, "X" on the floor, falling piano, the whole bit. Hilarious. That was the springboard from

▲ PATCH ZIRCHER
▲ SHANE LAW

which I dived back into my own book—which was bad news for the Skrulls, Norman Osborn, the Thunderbolts, and the simian assassin (assassimian?) Hit-Monkey. Plus, if you've ever asked, "Hey, why isn't Deadpool an X-Man?"—and believe me, many have—the answer is here.

5 DEADPOOL MINIBUS HC
Deadpool Kills the Marvel Universe #1-4, Deadpool Killustrated #1-4, Deadpool Kills Deadpool #1-4, Night of the Living Deadpool #1-4, and Deadpool vs. Carnage #1-4

One Deadpool book on the stands just isn't enough. A guy like me needs room to breathe. Only a seemingly endless supply of shorter stories could possibly capture every facet of my winning personality—not to mention all those other Wade Wilsons across the Multiverse. That's why I had no option but to become Marvel's king of the limited series—with no small help from Cullen Bunn, who took the wheel for all the tales in this "Minibus." Sometimes, when Spidey says "no killing" for the 37th time that day, or when I look in the mirror and don't see Danny Rand's handsome mug smiling back, I fantasize about murderizing every last one of the oh-so-perfect cape-and-tights brigade. In this book, I do. Or a version of me does, at least. There's plenty of other carnage, too—and also Carnage—as only Cullen could capture it. Hail to the bus driver, bus driver, Bunn!

6 DEADPOOL BY POSEHN & DUGGAN OMNIBUS HC
Deadpool (2012) #1-45 and more!

I'm the wisecracking, smart-talking Merc with the Mouth who just won't quit. So putting my words on the page is the work of two men. Surprising it took so long, then, for Marvel

to hand my title to a comedy-writing team. But when they finally did, Brian Posehn and Gerry Duggan stepped forward to turn my world upside down. A secret daughter? A succubus queen for a wife? The darkest Deadpool tale ever told? These guys were supposed to be funny! Oh, wait, they were that, too. Not least in thinking they could turn in old inventory issues of Deadpool from the 1970s and '80s as their own work and get paid for it. What a pair of jokers!

7 DEADPOOL: BAD BLOOD OGN-HC

If you want to be taken seriously in the comics biz, you need to have a graphic novel. And my main man, Rob Liefeld, was just the guy to take me into the prestige format at long last (with help from Chris Sims and Chad Bowers). Thanks to the magic of flashbacks, Cable and his mutant Mouseketeers (you might remember them as X-Force) put in an appearance in an adventure that pits us against a new foe from my ever-murky past: Thumper. No, not the rabbit. Along the way, I jump rainbows on a freakin' unicorn. And you know how much I dig unicorns.

8 SPIDER-MAN/DEADPOOL BY JOE KELLY & ED McGUINNESS HC
Spider-Man/Deadpool #1-5, #8-10, #13-14 and #17-18, on sale in March 2018!

Never go back, they say. Screw that, say Joe Kelly and Ed McGuinness. The duo who cemented my place as one of the greatest characters in comics returned to do the same thing for Spider-Man—and I was only too happy to help out a friend. If you like your action with a heaping helping of bromance, this is the one for you. Spidey and I make for one hell of a double act—with Webs as the straight man, obvs. But prepare to be freaked out when our psycho "daughter," Itsy Bitsy, crawls up the water spout—she has the daddy issues to end all daddy issues. Whole long boxes full of 'em!

9 DESPICABLE DEADPOOL
Beginning with Despicable Deadpool #287 in October 2017!

Which brings us all the way up to Marvel Legacy—and if anyone's the physical embodiment of that, then it's Deadpool! Let's take a little look-see at that checklist on page 7 and see what they have planned for my book... Wait a minute. "Despicable"—me? I'm loving the old-school alliteration, sure. And I dig the big number. But why not "Delightful Deadpool"? Or "Debonair Deadpool"? Or "Don't Give A @#$% What You Think Deadpool"? Anyway, sneaking a peek at Gerry Duggan's notes, it's gonna have old foes returning and "just wanting to get the hell out of Wade's orbit," while I'm my "own worst enemy." Well, maybe apart from Cable. Then there are these five words at the bottom that just sound like completely

unrelated-yet-useful advice: "Don't corner a wounded animal." Well, that's it from me—good luck building your very own Deadpool library. And if you want me to cut the ribbon when it's open, my rates are very reasonable.

Joe & Q&A

PHOTO BY MARYANN BATES

—— BY DUGAN TRODGLEN ——

After the industry-wide '90s bubble burst and Marvel filed for bankruptcy protection, the publisher's future appeared grim. One of the keys to emerging from bankruptcy was through innovations led by new President Bill Jemas and **Editor in Chief Joe Quesada**. Quesada was hired in 2000 after his own company, Event Comics (co-run by Jimmy Palmiotti), headed the well-received Marvel Knights imprint. Marvel Knights' approach and aesthetic was slowly adapted line-wide, and the publisher experienced a major resurgence. Quesada's tenure as EIC ended in 2011; he remains with the company as chief creative officer, with a hand not only in publishing, but other media as well—such as Marvel TV, the lineup of which includes his beloved Daredevil, the character with which he first made his mark at Marvel as editor and artist.

FOOM: You started at Marvel by editing a small, tight line of comics with the Marvel Knights imprint. Were you surprised to get that call, and by how much creative freedom you were given?

QUESADA: Yes and no. It was a surprise to get a call from Marvel President Joe Calamari ("Joey Squid") out of the blue. We weren't quite sure what he wanted to talk about, but he started by saying that Marvel was in dire straits. He said he really admired the way Jimmy and I ran our own publishing company, Event Comics. We were a three-person company with no money and managed to really get our stuff out there using sheer energy and guerilla tactics. The questions he left us with were, "If you could do anything at Marvel, what would you do? How would you see Marvel going forward with you guys involved that might help improve our business?"

We ran to my apartment and put together a plan that was pretty much exactly what happened. We knew we wanted *Daredevil* and didn't think that would be a problem: The book was on the verge of being canceled.

The Punisher had been canceled, and the Inhumans and Black Panther didn't have books. But my idea was to go back to Joey Squid and say, "Give us the whole line. Let us be co-editors in chief." I knew if we asked for four books, he might give us one or two—but if we asked for more than we wanted, we'd get what we did want. So we went in and said, "Give us the whole line." And Joe said, "How about four books?" [*Laughs.*]

FOOM: After a couple of years at Marvel Knights, you were promoted to editor in chief.

QUESADA: You can't really call it a promotion, because Event Comics was hired on a contract to do Marvel Knights. In essence, when I was offered the job, I was hired away from my own company.

FOOM: What did that move—hiring the co-editor of its most forward-looking line—tell you about Marvel's vision of itself?

QUESADA: That they were desperate! [*Laughs.*]

We often talk about the time period. It really

was the Wild West. With the exception of MK and some scattered projects here and there, everything was going down, and it was a struggle to sell anything. But those are the ebbs and flows of the comic-book industry that have been going on for decades. But this was probably the worst period we've ever, ever had.

So Marvel had this idea that they really wanted to shake things up. They had a guy in charge, Bill Jemas, who was a great risk-taker and in many ways a visionary. He took great chances—and the chances he took, part of which was making a change at EIC, seemed to work out. We teamed up to do some crazy stuff. Suddenly, sales started to tick up, and conventions that used to be ghost towns were full of people of all walks and sizes. So little by little, success started to come back.

FOOM: Aside from the ups and downs of the industry, another cycle seems to be between looking forward, trying new things, and looking back, drawing more on nostalgia and traditionalism. Right now, we seem to be in a cycle that does

JOE QUESADA, JIMMY PALMIOTTI & RICHARD ISANOVE ▲

Marvel Universe into something that could but didn't have to, move as a unit. There was greater interaction among titles, and eventually—the crossover-event concept returned—first with *House of M*, then culminating with the watershed success of *Civil War*. How did you know the time was right to make this move?

QUESADA: It was organic. When we decided to do the crossovers, we wanted to make sure that the main series itself was self-contained, and if we were going to have ancillary titles, that they are not necessary for the reader to grasp the main story. They should be satellite stories that play off of the core event, and hopefully deepen it. *Civil War* was, to me, the perfect construct for the kind of crossover we wanted to do from that point on. The smaller stories that could be told within that event really excited us and excited the creators. And when the creators are excited, they are going to do their absolute best work.

FOOM: Your tenure was also marked by the establishment of several publishing lines, none more significant than the Ultimate line. Was that in the works before you were EIC?

QUESADA: The timing was that Bill Jemas came on as VP while we were doing Marvel Knights, and he had this idea for this thing later called the Ultimate Universe. It was to be a separate universe geared toward younger readers, with a Ground Zero approach to our heroes. Then Bill started to meet with editors to put together sort of off-the-beaten-path creative teams to launch *Spider-Man* and *X-Men*, but the writers offered up were the same writers who were already on the regular books. So he came into my office and asked if we knew any newer writers that could fill these slots. At that time, I had just received a pack of independent comics from Brian Michael Bendis, who was not well known at the time. I had hired Brian to write *Daredevil*, so I showed his stuff to Bill and said, "This guy has a tremendous voice, and he might be your *X-Men* guy."

The next day he came in and said, "Love this guy. I want him on *Spider-Man*. Who do you have for *X-Men*?" [*Laughs.*] I told him about this guy Mark Millar and gave him some issues of the Wildstorm Comics series *The Authority* that featured some pretty out-there Avengers analogues in them. I knew he'd either be really offended or realize how amazingly talented this guy is. The next day he came in just over the moon, saying we had to get this guy for *X-Men*. At that point, Bill started bringing me in more and more for the Ultimate Universe meetings, and it was shortly after that that I was hired as EIC. And away we went.

FOOM: It goes without saying that trade paperbacks and other collected editions

---

incorporate nostalgia. What was it about the forward-looking approach that was so important at that time?

QUESADA: First, let me say that, as an industry, we have a very bad habit of always pointing at our own demise. Even when we're doing well, we wonder, "How much longer until it all collapses?"

Our goal at the start—mine, Bill's, all of the great writers and artists we worked with—was to bring in new readers and get them excited about comics, and to bring back lapsed readers. We did that by simplifying. When we came on board, Marvel was very continuity-driven. I remember reading one book in particular—I won't mention the title—but it was a 22-page comic, and 16 pages were flashbacks to previous things that happened to this character over the years. That was the world we were living in.

Now, probably the best comic of that period was Kurt Busiek and Alex Ross' *Marvels* [A

must-read look at the history of the Marvel Universe through the lens of photojournalist Phil Sheldon. -Ed.]. It's an absolute work of art, but it also tapped into a theme that was going on in comics at the time: It took you back to that classic time period. It gave a warm, glowing feeling to the older fan, like myself at the time, so I loved *Marvels*. What happened, though, is that the industry started doing a lot of books like that: books that looked backward instead of forward. And that's death, because you are sacrificing the new reader who might be coming in for the sake of the reader you already have, who will probably cycle out one day. Then you have neither reader. That is why it was so important to get away from telling stories that kept new readers at arm's length.

FOOM: Once you laid the foundation—making the books accessible, using continuity as a tool and not a crutch, keeping the titles fairly independent of one another—eventually you felt comfortable once again cohering the are a major component of comic-book publishing. How did you know that collected editions were the future?

QUESADA: All you had to do was do the math, but for some reason Marvel just didn't see it as a business model. All you had to do was look across town—not just at our rivals, but at Image, at Dark Horse. We were leaving money on the table. I guess the fear was that having trades would make people not want to buy the individual issues, and I guess that kind of made some sort of mathematical sense, but it didn't make sense to Bill and me.

Once the industry was driven by the direct market, the newsstand became the feeder that eventually got people into the comic shop. That was going the way of the dinosaur, and we needed a new feeder system. We figured that getting our product into other venues would only serve the direct market better by helping bring in new readers. And it did. It served Marvel tremendously. Look, this was not a genius move—it was an obvious move—but for some reason it was not obvious to Marvel at that time.

In a similar way, Marvel's coloring and production on their books, before Marvel Knights, was abysmal. Image was doing beautiful full-on computer coloring, as was my little company Event Comics. Marvel was still doing this old-school color that looked horrible next to the new techniques. One of the other stipulations I gave Bill when I was hired was that we had to go to computer coloring and better production.

FOOM: In 2001, Marvel abandoned the Comics Code Authority—the archaic self-regulation device created by the comics industry in the 1950s to appease the government. Eventually, the other publishers followed, and the CCA "stamp of approval" was replaced by ratings systems similar to video games or movies. I'm sure the decision to get out from under the CCA was easy, but was it difficult to make happen?

QUESADA: No! [*Laughs.*] Surprisingly not. I told Bill that we had to get out of it, and

at the time I had no idea what would be involved with doing so. I only knew I hated seeing that stamp. First of all, its history is an insidious one. Not only does it represent the government's attempt to censor creativity based on false information, but it also represented the industry just taking it. I mean, I didn't live in that time period, and they were trying to save the industry, but I hated everything about it every time I looked at it. And not only that, but we paid for the pleasure of being censored! We paid to have our books sent out and scoured, and sent back with notes to fix the most ridiculous things.

When I told Bill we had to get out of it, he just said, "Okay!" Mind you, this did not go down well with other publishers. DC contacted us, Archie Comics contacted us. Everyone was in a panic. So we had a fateful meeting in Marvel's conference room with the heads of Archie and DC. They were giving us a history lesson, and the Archie guys had a portfolio with yellowed newspaper clippings from the period. [*Laughs.*] I remember one of them pointed to one of the clippings and said, "See? If we don't stay with the Comics Code, senators will come after us!" While I was stifling a laugh, Bill looked at him and said, "Frankly, I'm more scared of Sentinels than I am of senators." [*Laughs.*] That was the end of the meeting. So we left the CCA, eventually DC and Archie did as well, and you know what happened? Nothing!

FOOM: Without tooting your own horn more than you are comfortable doing, what can you say about the difference between Marvel from the day you sat down in the EIC chair and the day you turned it over to Axel Alonso?

QUESADA: There are interviews from my early days on the job where I said my goal as editor in chief is to tell some great stories, not break anything, and hopefully leave things right where I found them, hopefully in better shape than when I found them. My other hope was that I would know when it was time to leave on my own. I was lucky enough for that to happen. I was given the position of chief creative officer while I was still EIC. And shortly after that, I talked to then-Publisher Dan Buckley and told him

▲ JOE QUESADA, DANNY MIKI & RICHARD ISANOVE

HOW "THE BOY" FOLLOWED "THE MAN"
ROY THOMAS LOOKS BACK ON HIS TIME AS EDITOR IN CHIEF
by Dugan Trodglen

When Stan Lee stepped aside as editor in chief in 1972, his natural successor was Roy Thomas, Marvel's most active writer at the time. Thomas was the first of his kind: a superfan turned creator, who grew up on comics and then turned that love into a profession. This provided him with an entirely different perspective than those who had come before—not only as a writer, but as an editor.

Thomas guided Marvel through the dawn of the "Bronze Age"—an era marked by line expansion; the acquisition of licensed titles such as *Star Wars* and *Conan the Barbarian* (the latter of which Thomas himself wrote for decades); the emergence of the All-New, All-Different X-Men; the introduction of new concepts including the Defenders, the Invaders, Ghost Rider, and *What If?*; the broadening of genres within publishing; and the influx of young, fresh blood into the Bullpen, which led to comics that were maturing with their audience.

....

FOOM: Before you were EIC, you led the wave of younger creators joining the Marvel Bullpen in the latter half of the '60s. How do you think that infusion of youth affected Marvel going forward?

Thomas: It gave Marvel (and DC, which also began to hire young artists and writers) a new lease on life, as the people who'd entered the field in the '40s (there'd been relatively few new guys since) were aging and new blood was needed. But then, it always is, isn't it?

FOOM: Replacing Stan, you didn't just have to fill the shoes of an iconic editor, but also the only EIC Marvel had had up to that point. What was the transition like?

Thomas: Stan just told me about the change, appointed me story editor (the EIC came a week or three later), and we got back to work. There were changes, but they didn't happen all at once. Stan was still in charge, still acting like the head editor, though as time went by his publishing duties grew and he came to leave more and more to me.

FOOM: Although you grew up the world's greatest super hero fan, you had a hand in expanding the concept to include horror characters such as Ghost Rider and the martial artist Iron Fist. What led to the diversification?

Thomas: We knew that we needed to appeal to more readers than just those of super hero comics. Of course, many super hero fans also liked Ghost Rider, Iron Fist, et al.—but we thought we might grab a few readers who were more interested in horror/supernatural or martial arts than in super heroes, and to some extent that worked. But they were still super hero comics, in their way.

FOOM: You engineered the incorporation of the *Star Wars* comic book into Marvel's publishing line. Much like today, it was a boon for the publisher, and Jim Shooter is quoted as saying Marvel "would have gone out of business" without the *Star Wars* license. Hyperbole aside, how did that affect Marvel?

Thomas: Jim probably meant what he said. I thought *Star Wars* might be a fun project to do when George Lucas' media projects director, Charles Lippincott, brought it to me in February 1976 (more than a year before the movie opened—it was only then beginning filming in North Africa). It turned out to make the company so much money in 1977–78 that it bought time for Marvel to make some moves to adjust to the changing realities of the comic-book marketplace amid high inflation, etc. Marvel's then president, James Galton, said of me to a mutual friend about a decade and a half ago: "He made me rich." So I assume that Jim's statement was not meant as hyperbole.

FOOM: Unlike today, editors and EICs were very active as writers as well during the '60s and '70s. How did that affect your role as EIC?

Thomas: It left me less time for it than I should have had, because I had to write on evenings and weekends. Small wonder I gave up after a bit over two years... and that none of my next four successors lasted as long as I had!

it was time for me to cycle out. It was time for someone new. We took a year to groom Axel, and I think that worked out great.

But as for my tenure, look, I was part of a tremendous team, a tremendous creative community. I was also lucky enough to be part of a very rare American success story: a company that went from nothing to exploding into popular culture with enormous success from the time of Stan Lee to the point when the company went public with its stock offerings, to then total collapse in the '90s. I was there as part of an incredible team to see it from collapse to resurgence—not just to where it was, but beyond, all the way to merging with a company like Disney. So I was very lucky to have been the one sitting in the chair, and to be able to move on within the company and hand the reins over to Axel of a company that I think was in better shape than when I started.

There is one thing that I think I can sort of toot my own horn about. When Stan Lee was in charge of the company, there was a real prominent, and vocal, face to the company. He gave the creators a face and a voice as well. We lost that after Stan. We didn't have someone who was really out there. That was something I wanted to bring back. I was really happy to be able to do that, to put a face on Marvel. And not just me, but the creators and editors as well. We really got out there and talked to fandom and helped create the kind of buzz that contributed to our success.

FOOM: Speaking of Stan, he is arguably the only EIC that had a greater impact than you on Marvel. Did you ever speak to Stan about the job or get advice?

QUESADA: Yes, absolutely. I would talk to Stan about Marvel and about our characters before I was editor in chief. I would cold-call Stan from the Marvel Knights office, and Marvel would be furious with me. "Who is this guy who's calling Stan?" [Laughs.] But no one else was calling him. I sent the outlines of the first four Marvel Knights books to Stan, and he gave me some notes on them, which was fantastic. And he was so happy to get them because he said that no one was sending him Marvel stuff. We would talk about how to create and build a perfect Marvel character. It was invaluable.

We talked sometimes about his EIC tenure, but it was such a different time. There were similarities in terms of plugging creators, the positive outlook, and keeping a cheery face regardless of what was happening, and the keeping in touch with fandom. But it was also different, because Stan was also writing all of those books! My job was a bit different. We were bailing water out of the ship. I had been a writer/artist before my tenure, so we were both creators—but to me Stan, along with Jack Kirby, is the greatest comic creator of all time.

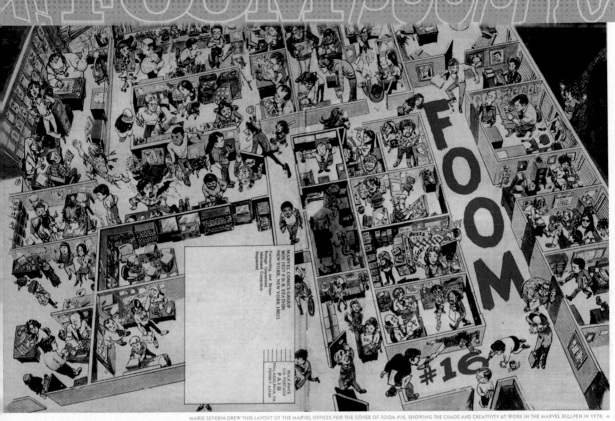

MARIE SEVERIN DREW THIS LAYOUT OF THE MARVEL OFFICES FOR THE COVER OF *FOOM #16*, SHOWING THE CHAOS AND CREATIVITY AT WORK IN THE MARVEL BULLPEN IN 1978. ▲

A STRETCH IN THE PEN

A (VERY) BRIEF HISTORY OF THE MARVEL BULLPEN

BY **JIM BEARD**

Stan Lee's penchant for distilling the magical from the mundane included the mythologizing of not only his writers and artists, but also the office staff responsible for the production of Marvel's comic books.

The so-called Marvel Bullpen was born out of necessity to conduct the business of publishing comics—though to Marvel's multitude of fans, eagerly devouring Lee's "Bullpen Bulletins" on the books' letters pages, one might think it sprang forth from his head not unlike the goddess Athena from Zeus' enlightened noggin.

The term "bullpen" is most notably associated with baseball, denoting the area in which relief pitchers warm up before entering the game. But in Stan Lee's "Bullpen Bulletins," he conjured up the image of artists and writers banding together to produce the best stories possible from their blood, sweat, and tears.

In the beginning, Lee was the Bullpen, for the most part. Next came Flo Steinberg, his "Gal Friday." Steinberg's standing cannot be diminished: The very idea of Marvel's office staff did not exist before her—and while she didn't write *Amazing Spider-Man* or draw *Avengers*, her spirit and work ethic set the tone for Bullpens to come, and persists to this day.

In the earliest days of Marvel, circa 1963, the Bullpen basically existed as a two-person operation: Lee was writer, editor, and art director; Steinberg was secretary and gatekeeper. Sol Brodsky would come into the cramped Marvel digs at 655 Madison Ave. to help with production, corrections, printing—the works—but was not yet a regular employee. That happy day came with a move up the street to 635 Madison Ave. and a bigger space—large enough for the two-person business to welcome a third cog into the machine. With Brodsky on staff, the three flew through their days at a frantic pace while other offices around them marveled at their efficiency and energy. It happened in one room—with a separate office for the editor, natch—and it shouldn't have worked. But somehow, it did.

As the Marvel line of titles grew, so did its Bullpen. Lee hired artist Marie Severin to assist Brodsky in production—she soon started on art chores as well—and from there the little company expanded to match the universe of super heroes within its publications. Before long, Lee, Brodsky, Steinberg and Severin welcomed letterers such as Art Simek and Sam Rosen into the furious fold, and they too were elevated into a kind of superstardom through Lee's perilous presentations of their personalities—artfully accentuated—in his "Bullpen Bulletins."

The end of the 1960s brought more change. Marvel switched printers, raised its 12-cent cover price to 15, and increased its output due to company owner Martin Goodman's deal with a new distributor. Despite the happy news behind the scenes, a note of sadness pervaded the Bullpen Bulletins when Lee announced the departure of stalwart Jack Kirby in early 1970.

Throughout the 1960s, Marvel saw even more new employees cross its threshold.

Artist John Romita Sr., who had worked for Lee in the 1950s, had thought he was done with comics, but Lee persuaded him to come aboard anyway. Most famously, he took over *Amazing Spider-Man* after Steve Ditko's departure. But he had a role behind the scenes as well.

"I asked Stan if I could work in the Bullpen a couple of days a week because I couldn't get my work done at home with two kids," Romita recalls. "That quickly became four, then five days, and then Stan began using me as a correction artist, which shortly led to me becoming a sort of 'art director.' Gradually, I began giving young artists Stan's take on the Marvel Way to tell a story with pictures... Thirty years slipped by. Sounds impossible."

THIS KEY SHOWS WHO THE PLAYERS WERE ON THE FLOOR OF THE MARVEL BULLPEN IN 1978. ▲

As the Swingin' Seventies came around, the Bullpen became a training ground for new recruits at Marvel's new digs at 575 Madison Ave., and the production team found room there to spread out and perhaps discover desks of their own.

In 1972, when "The Man" finally accepted a somewhat-higher office as president and publisher, Marvel's then-40 books fell under the ever-watchful eye of Romita, its first art director beyond Lee himself.

Romita made it a family affair roughly 10 years into his tenure when his wife, Virginia, started helping him with filing and correspondence. Like many at Marvel, the part-time position grew into full-time work, and the Romita duo saw another 20 years pass working together.

"The time flew by, and it led to great times and innovations like Romita's Raiders," the artist notes, pointing out his personal team of production assistants who ran "raids" on aspects of the art that needed either a gentle nudge or sometimes a big push to fall into line. "We gave young artists a chance to learn how to tell stories the Marvel Way. One of those with talent stood out: John Romita Jr. I was also there to do many promotional projects like the Macy's Thanksgiving Day Parade balloon, coloring books, etc."

Luminaries such as John Verpoorten—who later became production manager—Morrie Kuramoto, Frank Giacoia, and Mike Esposito worked side by side in the office with the Romitas to keep the Marvel engine chugging along, and ensuring a look and style to the titles that Lee had inaugurated years before.

Many longtime Marvel Bullpenners can trace the lineage of their comic-book careers back to the Romitas' tutelage among the "Raiders."

Severin somehow captured the zeitgeist of those days in one amazing drawing. In 1976, for the sixteenth issue of FOOM, she laid out what was basically a caricature of the Marvel offices and its denizens. In the sprawling, somewhat irreverent view of the House of Ideas' rooms and hallways, nearly every employee could be seen creating the chaos that all Marvel fans knew went on each day there. Now fans had a visual document to cement the fantasy life of the Bullpen in their fevered brains.

In 1978, after a steady profusion of editors in chief following Lee's departure, Marvel promoted editor Jim Shooter to the position, and the Marvel Universe would never be the same as it headed into another new decade. Lee moved to Los Angeles in 1980 to work on larger projects such as Marvel films and TV shows. Business continued, but not always as usual. Shooter reinstated a throwback Bullpen Bulletins in the comics in 1981, a column more like Lee's with mentions of weddings and promotions, births and deaths. One of those passings was that of longtime Bullpenner Kuramoto in 1985.

New World Pictures purchased Marvel in 1986; by the next year, Shooter was out as editor in chief, and Tom DeFalco was in. Together with new Executive Editor Mark Gruenwald, DeFalco oversaw another increase in the number of Marvel books on the stands, as well as maintaining the Bullpen Bulletins page to ensure that Marvel's personalities would continue to receive their due.

Among those Bullpen personalities was Dan Crespi, a letterer and inker who went on to become production manager until his death in 1985. His daughter, Susan, cites her father as the reason she has "comics in my blood."

"Growing up, he would always tell stories of Bullpen life, and it sounded like a fun place to work," Crespi says. "After college, I worked as a calligrapher in a scroll studio until I was let go in the early '90s. That fateful day I ran into my cousin, Nel Yomtov, on the subway platform. He was working as an editor at Marvel. I told him what had transpired, and he set up an introduction with one of the letterers, Jim Novak, who then trained me. When Jim felt I was ready, I was able to get my first freelance gig. A few months later, there was an opening in the Bullpen for a staff letterer—and 25 years later, I'm still here.

"During office hours, I did lettering corrections, cover copy, and designed logos, all by hand as it was before the digital age. Once computers came into the picture, my role changed to digital compositor. I worked my way up to supervising the Bullpen and the freelance letterers as the production manager. My job these days is more administrative than anything else. I work closely with other departments to make sure that systems are running smoothly, and that files go to press and are print-ready. I troubleshoot problems that arise at the eleventh hour."

Crespi says her greatest joy as a Bullpenner comes from being in a position to give others the chance to break into the business. "I feel like in some small way I'm able to give back the opportunity that was given to me," she says.

The dawn of the 1990s offered up a new Marvel president, Ron Perelman, and the happy occasion of a sales spike.

Another 1990s entrant into the hallowed halls of the House of Ideas and the cattle call of the Bullpen was artist Scott Kolins. After receiving a referral from fellow artist Bob Layton for an interview with John Romita, Kolins was offered a spot on the corrections team once its head man viewed his portfolio.

"Besides the advantage of being in the Marvel offices every day and being able to ask the John Romita questions and for tips," Kolins says of his Bullpen time, "John was truly one of the nicest guys in comics."

While much of the work could be uninspiring—minor corrections to larger pieces of art—Kolins relished the moments when he could do bigger work.

"There are two pieces of art I happily remember working on...a couple of Michael Golden *Doctor Strange* and *Ghost Rider* covers that needed the empty old corner UPC box filled in [with art] because Marvel was making a poster book from them, and putting white dotted Zip-A-Tone over an Alan Davis–Mark Farmer *Excalibur* cover."

Kolins found that while his position essentially consisted of support work, there were times when he could fight for artistic integrity.

"One Michael Golden piece was especially cool for me because the editor wanted a whole leg redrawn as he thought Golden had drawn it poorly," Kolins says. "I went up the chain of command to complete the leg and its boot as Michael had intended—to the best of my ability—not how the junior editor wanted it. You don't 'fix' Michael Golden!"

The times were definitely a-changin'. Marvel declared bankruptcy in 1996, but saw a kind of white knight charge up in the form of new owner ToyBiz in 1998. In-house, the old ways of T-squares, paste-ups, and white correction fluid were giving way to state-of-the-art computer software, which of course prompted the Marvel Bullpen to up its game to stay current and increase efficiency.

Dan Carr recalls those times as exciting, when new technology meant new ways to do better work.

"Longtime friend and colleague Chris Eliopoulos was able to get me an interview on April Fool's Day, 1991," Carr says. "I was hired by Virginia Romita as the nighttime typesetter that day. And I became a full-time staffer on September 23rd. I had the first Macintosh computer in the publishing department—the desktop-publishing era had recently begun—and we spearheaded all digital processes for manufacturing a comic, from scanning and coloring, to lettering and printing, etc. I was eventually promoted from production manager to production director."

Carr says one of the real joys of his position was being able to create the production workflows that the company uses to this day. "There are many talented individuals in the comics industry, and I was able to give many their start in the Marvel Bullpen," he says proudly. "I continue to watch in awe the talent in this industry, and I am grateful that Marvel has allowed me to do so for so long."

Today, Carr is Marvel's executive director of publishing technology, which sounds like a far cry from the days of a single room crammed with production assistants. Eliopoulos now runs Virtual Calligraphy, the company that letters the majority of Marvel's books, another change from a time when all lettering was done by hand and in-house. Chief among those who developed that in-house lettering system was Dave Sharpe.

"I came on staff under Virginia Romita in 1990 into the lettering section of the Bullpen," Sharpe says. "Everything was still being done by hand, and my job was to mimic lettering styles and do corrections on the lettering, which would be on overlays, or the actual art—back when lettering was actually done on the art boards! Around the year 2000, computers and fonts were introduced to comics, and I helped develop a lettering department. A few years later, lettering became fully outsourced.

"Learning the lettering-by-hand skill, and then evolving to computer lettering, and then continuing to letter in this business is a huge deal to me. And working alongside *legends* like John Romita Sr. and Michael Golden was a dream come true."

The new millennium brought even more fresh faces to the Bullpen as Marvel merrily marched into yet another exciting era with new Editor in Chief Joe Quesada and new President Bill Jemas. Among the those fresh faces of 2001 was writer, editor, and novelist Bob Greenberger, who felt the weight of history in the position he'd taken on, despite the stretch of years between him and those nascent days of Stan and Flo and Sol.

"One of the thrills about being hired at Marvel was that I would be tasked with overseeing the fabled Bullpen," he says. "Back in the 1960s, it was a tiny operation since there were just a few titles. When I got there, the company was putting out something like 60 titles, and the Bullpen had about a dozen people plus an in-house lettering department, which I would eventually come to oversee as well. It was also a time of transition as digital corrections and receipt of digital art files was becoming more commonplace.

"I was hired as director of publishing operations, and production was part of my initial portfolio. Many of the faces around me were young and incredibly enthusiastic, hardworking people who grew up as comics fans, as thrilled as I was to be working there. Anchoring the department's history was Assistant Production Manager Susan Crespi, whose father, Danny, was Marvel's art/production supervisor.

"Once I gained the lettering team, we began designing a digital workflow to make it easier for pages to go from editorial to proofreading—the lovely, late Flo Steinberg—to production to the printer."

Today, the Marvel Bullpen operates in a world perhaps undreamt of by its founders nearly 60 years ago. Writers and artists who ply their trade almost solely within the realm of computers, and those who receive their work and move it into production and publication do the same.

The Bullpen rolled with the times and worked according to the technology and the limitations of each decade. The end result is the same: Comics are comics, and the reader enjoys them whether or not they are aware of the men and women behind the scenes who make them happen.

However, thanks to Stan Lee's myth-making magic and the spirit of its denizens, the Bullpen will always retain an air of chaos and creativity in the Hallowed Halls of the House of Ideas.

▲ THE BULLPEN AS IT EXISTED IN MARVEL'S EARLY DAYS, AS SEEN IN THIS LAYOUT FROM 1969'S *FANTASTIC FOUR ANNUAL #7*.

BY JOHN RHETT THOMAS

THE INSPIRATION OF THE OFFICE

Flo served as a proofreader upon her return to Marvel in the 1990s, a job she held until she passed away this July. Along the way, she served as a coworker, friend, and mentor to countless Bullpenners. **Jacque Porte**, *who joined Marvel as a proofreader in December 2014, was one of them.*

Fabulous Flo arrived at the end of my exhausting first week at Marvel, gave me a hug and a big wet kiss, and told me how excited she was to work with me. Imagine that! As if I were the one with the storied career and myriad accomplishments! She set herself up behind me with her giant headphones, her oversized sweatshirt and glasses, and an egg sandwich, and murmured away while she proofed the fantastical adventures of characters she had watched come to life decades before.

Her presence had a marked effect on the office. Even passing in the hallway, she could be depended upon for a humorous comment or a kind word, and her ability to remember even the most subtle detail made her an amazing proofreader and an even better friend. I don't think she realized just how broad her reach extended. She inspired me, helped foster my frustration into something productive, and encouraged my efforts to create an atmosphere of friendly teamwork with the other departments.

She made proofreading into a team sport. We argued over points of grammar, giggled over amusing errors (she'd underline your/you're errors at least five times), and mooned over the Punisher (she was quite fond of Frank's strong jawline, and the fact that his books were more sound effects than text didn't hurt his appeal either).

Now she sits behind me in memory, bent over the latest proof, and I can only hope to carry on her legacy of making every book a little bit better, every soul a little bit brighter.

In the Marvel Universe, there was a galaxy. And in that galaxy was a planet. And on that planet was a city. And in that city was a comic-book publisher. And in that comic-book publisher's office were three people: one editing, one in charge of production, and one so fabulous they capitalized the word whenever they affixed it to her name. And that woman was one of the most important women in Marvel Comics history, which—let's be honest—makes her one of the most important women in comics history. That woman's name was Flo Steinberg—and that's *Fabulous* Flo to you and everyone who ever had the pleasure of meeting her.

In the spring of 1963, the Marvel Comics office at 625 Madison Ave. was hardly the center of any kind of grand, interconnected universe. That would come later. It was a two-person operation run by Stan Lee, the editor in chief, and Sol Brodsky, the man who could do it all in production—and *had to* because he was the only one around to do it! The pair often played host to a gaggle of talented artists (at that time, legendary names such as Kirby, Ditko, and Heck, among others) who mostly worked from home, only visiting the office to turn in pages, review plotlines with Stan, and maybe do a little drawing as needed.

But Stan was having problems. Mind you, they were the kinds of problems that were born of success: *Fantastic Four #1* had appeared in comics racks the summer of 1961 and been the kind of hit that pumped new life into the fading company. The FF was soon followed by a host of new super heroes: Ant-Man, Thor, Hulk, Spider-Man, and Iron Man, all with titles that needed to be written and drawn and delivered to the printer on time. And each new character brought in a boatload of enthusiastic new fan mail Stan felt compelled to reply to in person. Marvel's fortunes were on a steep upward curve, and Stan needed someone to help him manage the office so he could focus on the creative side of things.

And that's when Florence Steinberg walked through the door. An employment agency sent her over to interview with Stan, who had solicited a position for a "girl Friday," a term popularized by the 1940 film *His Girl Friday* starring Cary Grant and Rosalind Russell. At age 25, Flo could scarcely guess what she was walking into. Born and raised in Boston, and schooled at University of Massachusetts in Amherst, she had a history degree under her belt when she decided to move to the Big Apple and establish her future. She didn't know precisely what she wanted to do with her life, only that like so many "career girls" of the time she wanted to do it in New York City.

Her immediate concerns on the job were secretarial in nature: answering phones, reaching out to printers, consulting with engravers, and checking in with freelancers on their deadlines. Surely, her charm and perky sensibility helped smooth over any rough edges of the daily grind of putting out comic books on time. It also helped in the kind of secretarial duties nobody could have prepared her for: dealing with the fans!

The deluge of fan mail needed answering, and every day it seemed to be increasing. Stan couldn't keep up with the amount of correspondence he had been doing; he also felt that connecting with readers of his expanding universe of comic books was of key importance to the company's future. So that responsibility shifted over to Flo, who would go on to answer thousands (tens of thousands?) of letters that arrived in the office on a daily basis. Stan hit pay dirt with Flo's affable, fandom-friendly personality. She truly was a mirror image of his own enthusiasm and ability for reaching out to fans in the Marvel Age way. No stuffy, punch-the-clock secretary was she!

Through Stan and Flo's efforts, the small three-man office was mythologized into a hustling, bustling Bullpen of madcap creativity. The kind of office environment that enlivened the imaginations of readers already sent into far-out realms by the cutting-edge adventures of their Marvel heroes. It was indeed all part of Stan's plan: to create a passionate, personal relationship between readers and the line of comics they had embraced. And Flo helped steer the ship.

Meanwhile, some of her duties truly were of the "Batty Bullpen" variety, one famous example being her facility with an ashtray whenever artist Wallace Wood visited Stan's office. The chain-smoker routinely—and some would say passive-aggressively—ignored the ashtrays available to him and dropped ashes on the carpeting in Stan's office. Flo would be right there to inconspicuously set an ashtray under his cigarette whenever the ash was getting long and droopy. She also had to run interference on fans who called to talk to Stan, or arrived at the office unannounced to get a word in with Stan, or lurked around the elevators to just *please, please, let me tell Stan how much I love Marvel!* Not to mention fielding phone calls from fans who simply fell in love with her and wanted to yak it up with the

▲ COLLEEN COOVER

Fabulous gal who was at the center of their beloved Bullpen.

And in 1965, two years after her arrival, when Stan formed the Mighty Marvel Marching Society (MMMS) to harness the fandom that had reached critical mass, it was Flo who made sure all the club's goodies—from membership cards to a vinyl flexi disc record of the Bullpen talking and singing to their legions of fans—got in the mail and out to everyone who had ordered one. Membership of the MMMS reportedly grew to 50,000, each one considering Flo a superstar of the Bullpen firmament.

Stan once came up with a description of Flo in one of the credits boxes in a Marvel annual: "Flo Steinberg— Exasperated Example of Secretarial Suffering." Later in the decade, Fabulous Flo left the job she'd held for five years. Sure, her position had been "secretary," but that was only because "Center of Gravity of the Marvel Universe" hadn't existed before her arrival.

After Marvel, Flo held various jobs inside and outside the comics and publishing industries. She even developed her own underground comic magazine, *Big Apple Comix* (which featured cover art from the ash-dropping Wood). She lived on in Marvel Comics through various cameos, the most famous being a role as the Invisible Woman in a Kirby-written-and-drawn issue of *What If?* She returned to Marvel in the '90s to serve as a proofreader, a position she held for the rest of her life.

Sadly, we write this article as a eulogy. Flo passed away on July 23, 2017, from complications from a brain aneurysm and metastatic lung cancer. Tributes flowed in from all corners of the comic-book industry and fandom. Perhaps the most fitting thing one could say of Fabulous Flo comes from the mouth of her boss and fandom mentor, Stan Lee. When someone would bring up her name, the first thing out of Stan's mouth would often be: "Flo…what a gal!"

She was all that and plenty more. Rest in peace, Flo Steinberg.

THE STEALTH PHILOSOPHER

Linda Fite arrived at Marvel in the late 1960s to perform various tasks in the Bullpen, but was soon writing stories that appeared in various Western titles, X-Men, and The Cat. She also contributed to Flo's Big Apple Comix. Fite married longtime Incredible Hulk and G.I. Joe artist Herb Trimpe, and started a family with him while also working for 20 years as a staff writer for the Times Herald-Record in Middletown, New York. Through it all, she remained the closest of friends with Flo.

"Fabulous Flo" is right.

I was hired, at Flo's behest, to help her with the increasing influx of fan mail, as well as all sorts of other "editorial/production" assistance I could offer. She reached out to me (by letter, then by phone) after I wrote to Marvel asking for a job. (I still have a copy of that letter, as well as Flo's response, encouraging me to come talk to Stan after I moved to New York City, without a promise of a job, but with plenty of hope thereof.) One thing that cracks me up, in retrospect, is that Stan had circled the sentence "I can type" in my letter!

As anyone who ever spent more than a minute with her knows, Flo was incredibly kind, incredibly "nice" to everyone. And that made my first post-college job so easy (that and the genial atmosphere of the Bullpen).

We were close friends ever since that time. She was my son's godmother! And she loved and showered affection on all three of the kids born to me and Herb.

I have scads of anecdotes, of course, but most of them are...I dunno... not very "pithy" and maybe not so appropriate for print! But after going through her effects as her executor, I came across a small, cloth-bound notebook in which she had written or photocopied dozens and dozens of quotes or passages, short and long, from authors, wits, and wags— people whose thoughts tickled her or impressed her or made her say (to herself, presumably), "Damn right!"

A rather telling number of these quotations had to do with mortality or solitude or courage. Here are a few:

"The cherry blossom falls from the tree with the first strong breeze, but we do not say that it has never lived. A bloom that lasts only a day is no less beautiful for that."
– *Shike: Last of the Zinja* by Robert Shea

"Time is the random wind that blows down the long corridor, slamming all the doors."
– *A Tan and Sandy Silence* by John D. MacDonald

"To see what is right and not to do it is want of courage."
– Confucius

"Love consists in this—that two solitudes protect and touch and greet one another."
– Rilke

"Do not desire that everything happen as you wish, but desire that everything happen as in fact it does happen, and you will be free."
– Epictetus

"To be attached to the subdivision, to love the little platoon we belong to in society, is the first principle (the germ as it were) of public affections. It is the first link in the series by which we proceed toward a love to our country, and to mankind."
– Edmund Burke

"...Life is hard and getting no easier. But there are exceptions, moments of, if not hope, at least relief. A child is born healthy. A book absorbs us. A friend laughs. Unwanted guests depart and never return."
– Spoken by the character Rostnikov in *Death of a Russian Priest* by Stuart M. Kaminsky

All these quotes were very much Flo: the ponderer, the thinker, the stealth philosopher. Wise, funny, intelligent, fun, loyal, considerate— fabulous.

MIGHTY MARVEL MINI-ITEMS

VALUE STAMPS CAN'T BE LICKED!
Break out your scissors, Marvel Mavens! A brand-new array of Marvel Value Stamps are coming your way courtesy of Marvel Legacy! For those of you asking, "What the heck is a 'Marvel Value Stamp'?"—the small, stamp-shaped curiosities, emblazoned with portraits of Marvel's most famous heroes and villains, appeared in select Marvel comics from 1974–1976. Just over 30 years later, *Marvel Spotlight* revived the concept, publishing a new slate of Value Stamps. And now comes Marvel Legacy, bringing with it 53 stamps illustrated by Mike McKone! Be sure to ask your local comic store for a copy of the free Marvel Stamp Collector Album, available Nov. 1st—then get clipping, True Believer!

▲ MIKE McKONE & RACHELLE ROSENBERG

◄ DAVID NAKAYAMA

AN ISSUE OF CLOSURE
Think your beloved *Not Brand Echh* collection is complete? Guess again! A mere 48 years after issue #13—how's that for a shipping delay?—the unforgettable Forbush Man makes his triumphant return as issue #14 finally sees print! It's one of a number of dearly departed titles from yesteryear returning as part of Marvel Legacy for one final issue—for now, at least! Say goodbye all over again with *Silver Sable & the Wild Pack* #36, *Power Pack* #63, *Darkhawk* #51, *Master of Kung Fu* #126—and, of course, *Not Brand Echh* #14.

THE LEGACY PITCH
FOOM grabbed hold of a handful of writers passing through the batty Bullpen and urged them to hit us with the quick pitch for their upcoming Marvel Legacy storylines—and this is what they threw our way!

Max Bemis on *Moon Knight*: "If Moon Knight is a Batman for the unhinged, who would his Joker be? Moon Knight fights his new archnemesis for the fate of creativity and freedom itself."

Victor Gischler on *Spirits of Vengeance*: "When a third-rate sorcerer looks to make a name for himself, he discovers how to weaponize the 30 pieces of silver paid to Judas for betraying Jesus. What is the only answer for the ultimate betrayal? The ultimate vengeance, of course."

Margaret Stohl on *Captain Marvel*: "When Captain Marvel discovers an Upside-Down Earth—where she is a super villain called the Private, and the Zeta are her criminal crew—she finds herself caught in the crosshairs of a deadly intergalactic assassin: Peter Quill, also known as Lord Starkill!"

Rodney Barnes on *Falcon*: "In the aftermath of Secret Empire, Sam Wilson seeks to reconnect with grassroots America—only to find Blackheart standing in his way!"

▲ JESÚS SAIZ

OPTIMUM PRIMERS
Want a refresher course in the history of Marvel's colorful cast of costumed characters? We have you covered! The first issue of each Legacy title will feature three page "Primers," written by Robbie Thompson and—in many cases—drawn by the incomparable Mark Bagley. "When I first approached Robbie and Mark to do these Primer stories, I gave them only one edict," editor Darren Shan said. "To remind all readers both who these characters are and what they're about in three all-new pages. What we got back has been some of the most fun art I've ever seen from Mark! And we couldn't be luckier to have someone like Robbie to cherry-pick the most classic moments in Marvel history. The two of them tie this all up into one perfect package." Speaking of perfect packages, there's a good chance all the Marvel Legacy Primer pages will be collected in a single trade paperback in the near future—so keep your eyes peeled!

▲ MARK BAGLEY, JOHN DELL & RACHELLE ROSENBERG

PERIODICALS OF TERROR!
Did you know Marvel once graced the newsstands as well as the comics racks? *Marvel Horror: The Magazine Collection TPB* collects the most horrifying stories of the 1970s magazines. Blade, Satana, and Gabriel, Devil Hunter, join a selection of scary stories for the Halloween season. Pick it up in stores everywhere Oct. 11th.

GENE COLAN & JUSTIN PONSOR ▲

MARVEL UNIVERSE

001

MARVEL LEGACY #1 VARIANT BY **MARK BROOKS**

MARVEL LEGACY #1 VARIANT BY **MIKE DEODATO JR.**

ALL-NEW WOLVERINE #25
LEGACY HEADSHOT VARIANT BY
MIKE McKONE & RACHELLE ROSENBERG

AMERICA #8
LEGACY HEADSHOT VARIANT BY
MIKE McKONE & ANDY TROY

AMAZING SPIDER-MAN #789
LEGACY HEADSHOT VARIANT BY
MIKE McKONE & RACHELLE ROSENBERG

AMAZING SPIDER-MAN: RENEW YOUR VOWS #13
LEGACY HEADSHOT VARIANT BY
MIKE McKONE & RACHELLE ROSENBERG

AVENGERS #672
LEGACY HEADSHOT VARIANT BY

ASTONISHING X-MEN #7
LEGACY HEADSHOT VARIANT BY
MIKE McKONE & RACHELLE ROSENBERG

BLACK BOLT #8
LEGACY HEADSHOT VARIANT BY
MIKE McKONE & RACHELLE ROSENBERG

BLACK PANTHER #166
LEGACY HEADSHOT VARIANT BY
MIKE McKONE & RACHELLE ROSENBERG

BEN REILLY: SCARLET SPIDER #10
LEGACY HEADSHOT VARIANT BY
MIKE McKONE & ANDY TROY

CABLE #150
LEGACY HEADSHOT VARIANT BY
MIKE McKONE & RACHELLE ROSENBERG

CAPTAIN AMERICA #695
LEGACY HEADSHOT VARIANT BY
MIKE McKONE & RACHELLE ROSENBERG

CAPTAIN MARVEL #125
LEGACY HEADSHOT VARIANT BY
MIKE McKONE & RACHELLE ROSENBERG

CHAMPIONS #13
LEGACY HEADSHOT VARIANT BY
MIKE McKONE & RACHELLE ROSENBERG

DAREDEVIL #595
LEGACY HEADSHOT VARIANT BY
MIKE McKONE & RACHELLE ROSENBERG

DESPICABLE DEADPOOL #287
LEGACY HEADSHOT VARIANT BY
MIKE McKONE & RACHELLE ROSENBERG

DOCTOR STRANGE #381
LEGACY HEADSHOT VARIANT BY
MIKE McKONE & RACHELLE ROSENBERG

FALCON #1
LEGACY HEADSHOT VARIANT BY
MIKE McKONE & RACHELLE ROSENBERG

GENERATION X #85
LEGACY HEADSHOT VARIANT BY
MIKE McKONE & ANDY TROY

GUARDIANS OF THE GALAXY #146
LEGACY HEADSHOT VARIANT BY
MIKE McKONE & RACHELLE ROSENBERG

HAWKEYE #13
LEGACY HEADSHOT VARIANT BY

ICEMAN #6
LEGACY HEADSHOT VARIANT BY
MIKE McKONE & ANDY TROY

INCREDIBLE HULK #709
LEGACY HEADSHOT VARIANT BY
MIKE McKONE & RACHELLE ROSENBERG

INVINCIBLE IRON MAN #593
LEGACY HEADSHOT VARIANT BY
MIKE McKONE & RACHELLE ROSENBERG

IRON FIST #73
LEGACY HEADSHOT VARIANT BY
MIKE McKONE & ANDY TROY

JEAN GREY #8
LEGACY HEADSHOT VARIANT BY
MIKE McKONE & ANDY TROY

JESSICA JONES #13
LEGACY HEADSHOT VARIANT BY
MIKE McKONE & ANDY TROY

LUKE CAGE #166
LEGACY HEADSHOT VARIANT BY
MIKE McKONE & RACHELLE ROSENBERG

MARVEL 2-IN-ONE #1
LEGACY HEADSHOT VARIANT BY
MIKE McKONE & RACHELLE ROSENBERG

MOON GIRL AND DEVIL DINOSAUR #25
LEGACY HEADSHOT VARIANT BY
MIKE McKONE & ANDY TROY

MOON KNIGHT #188
LEGACY HEADSHOT VARIANT BY
MIKE McKONE & RACHELLE ROSENBERG

MS. MARVEL #25
LEGACY HEADSHOT VARIANT BY
MIKE McKONE & ANDY TROY

OLD MAN LOGAN #31
LEGACY HEADSHOT VARIANT BY
MIKE McKONE & RACHELLE ROSENBERG

PETER PARKER: THE SPECTACULAR SPIDER-MAN #297
LEGACY HEADSHOT VARIANT BY
MIKE McKONE & RACHELLE ROSENBERG

PUNISHER #218
LEGACY HEADSHOT VARIANT BY
MIKE McKONE & RACHELLE ROSENBERG

ROYALS #9
LEGACY HEADSHOT VARIANT BY
MIKE McKONE & RACHELLE ROSENBERG

SECRET WARRIORS #8
LEGACY HEADSHOT VARIANT BY
MIKE McKONE & ANDY TROY

SHE-HULK #159
LEGACY HEADSHOT VARIANT BY
MIKE McKONE & RACHELLE ROSENBERG

SPIDER-MAN #234
LEGACY HEADSHOT VARIANT BY
MIKE McKONE & ANDY TROY

SPIDER-MAN/DEADPOOL #23
LEGACY HEADSHOT VARIANT BY
MIKE McKONE & RACHELLE ROSENBERG

SPIRITS OF VENGEANCE #1
LEGACY HEADSHOT VARIANT BY
MIKE McKONE & RACHELLE ROSENBERG

TALES OF SUSPENSE #100
LEGACY HEADSHOT VARIANT BY
MIKE McKONE & RACHELLE ROSENBERG

UNBEATABLE SQUIRREL GIRL #27
LEGACY HEADSHOT VARIANT BY
MIKE McKONE & ANDY TROY

UNBELIEVABLE GWENPOOL #21
LEGACY HEADSHOT VARIANT BY
MIKE McKONE & RACHELLE ROSENBERG

UNCANNY AVENGERS #28
LEGACY HEADSHOT VARIANT BY
MIKE McKONE & ANDY TROY

U.S.AVENGERS #11
LEGACY HEADSHOT VARIANT BY
MIKE McKONE & RACHELLE ROSENBERG

VENOM #155
LEGACY HEADSHOT VARIANT BY
MIKE McKONE & RACHELLE ROSENBERG

WEAPON X #12
LEGACY HEADSHOT VARIANT BY
MIKE McKONE & ANDY TROY

X-MEN BLUE #13
LEGACY HEADSHOT VARIANT BY
MIKE McKONE & RACHELLE ROSENBERG

X-MEN GOLD #13
LEGACY HEADSHOT VARIANT BY
MIKE McKONE & RACHELLE ROSENBERG